OUR REAL WAR:

WHAT HAPPENED TO AMERICA

M. J. MURPHY

ISBN: 1466487976

ISBN 13: 9781466487970

Library of Congress Control Number: 2011960031
CreateSpace Independent Publishing Platform
North Charleston, South Carolina

I would like to thank God for giving me the desire and fortitude to envision and complete this book. I would also like to thank God for placing the right people at the right time to help encourage me and correct my missteps. Vince and Tom, your help has meant more to me than you can know.

Introduction

With the 2008 financial crisis, America has suffered the worst economic downturn since the Great Depression. With unemployment that peaked at 10 percent in 2009, and increasing numbers of Americans needing government assistance, politicians spent trillions of dollars trying to jump-start the economy. Despite the enormous amounts of money that the government infused into the economy, the average American still feels pain. *Our Real War: What Happened to America* shows how America's economy can get much worse and provides a foundation to prevent it.

Our Real War: What Happened to America details the reasons the town of Millinocket, in north central Maine, was once called "The Magic City" and how it reached 30 percent unemployment a generation later. Millinocket and the neighboring communities of East Millinocket and Medway, which form the Katahdin-Three, are a microcosm of America. These three small towns epitomized what made America great, and have suffered unemployment levels greater than those of the Depression era as a result of the self-preservationist behavior of big government, big labor, and big business. The book goes on to examine the arc of General Motors (GM), which bears a surprising number of similarities to the economic collapse of Millinocket. The lessons we have learned from the experiences of General Motors and Millinocket provide a foundation from which to build a better America.

Millinocket and East Millinocket were created by Great Northern Paper Company (GNP). GNP built the towns around its mammoth paper mills in the middle of the rugged north Maine woods. The vast forest and hydro system that GNP was able to harness made the company impossible to fail, but yet it did. The economic fallout decimated the town. Likewise, a generation ago, GM was considered too massive and powerful to go bankrupt, but yet it did. Had the US government not provided funding to rescue GM after its bankruptcy, the economic fallout would have been enormous.

I feel blessed to have lived through the Katahdin-Three's economic collapse. The lessons learned in the darkest days of the Katahdin region's depression were magnified by the tragic General Motors bankruptcy. These events have helped me to see where America is headed. This nation need not suffer the fate that I have seen, but action needs to be taken now to avert America's demise. *Our Real War: What Happened to America* is the first step in taking back our country and placing it back on the path to prosperity.

Our Real War: What Happened to America will lay the groundwork for success at the personal, community, and national levels. By providing Americans with a sobering look into the nation's future, I hope to inspire people to embrace the virtues that made this nation great and to avoid the vices that caused the economic collapse of the Katahdin-Three and the bankruptcy of General Motors.

Contents

Chapter One

Millinocket, "The Magic City"

America is at war, and I have been on the front lines. The evil faces and soulless stares of the enemy send chills down my spine. The front lines of this war will take over major cities and small towns alike. Every American and every small business will eventually feel the ravages of this war. I am talking neither about any of our nation's historic military battles nor about the War on Terror. The war of which I speak is being waged against the American public by an axis of power seeking to sustain and grow its influence regardless of the consequences. The principles of big government, big labor, and big business are destroying this nation one community at a time; their self-indulgent behavior destroys everything in its path, and it will lead to the ruination of America.

An economic and historical analysis of my home town and one of America's greatest corporations illustrates the dire need for Americans to heed this warning. America used to be the beacon of hope to the poor and a lighthouse of opportunity to the entrepreneur. It has now been devastated by 10 percent unemployment; everyone knows of the sacrifices that businesses, communities, and citizens have been forced to make in order to survive. But imagine what it would be like to operate a small business in a community that had 30 percent unemployment and that was already economically decimated in the previous decade, a community that went from having one of the highest, if not the highest, per capita incomes in the state to losing almost half of its population a generation later.

I've had the privilege of doing just that. The town is real and the economy is scary. Words alone cannot adequately describe this community's journey from "The Magic City" to an American purgatory. There are striking similarities between what my town has gone through and where this country is going.

Senator Margaret Chase Smith, the late Maine Republican, once said, "Wake up, America." America needs to change its direction before it hits an iceberg and sinks. We, as a country, need to learn from the tragedy of my state and hometown in order to prevent the disease of decay from destroying our great country. My hometown did not participate in the tech boom of the 1990s nor in the housing boom of the 2000s, but we still suffered when each boom went bust. Yet we went from being the envy of the state to the joke of the state in just one generation. Our fate, as a community, was decided before anyone knew it. The brilliant planning of a few led to no planning by many, and thus our unenviable fate.

An Atmosphere for Growth

Maine separated from Massachusetts and became a state in 1820. Because of Maine's harsh climate and remote location, it lagged behind other states in growth despite homesteader programs designed to lure more people to the state. To help illustrate Maine's difficulties, the founder of the College of the Holy Cross, Benedict Joseph Fenwick, SJ, founded a small town just north of Millinocket called Benedicta. According to local residents, Fenwick's original intention for the tract of land was to lure people from the city to go to college. But the climate and location proved too formidable and he returned to Boston.

By the late 1800s, Maine was eager to develop its natural resources, and it encouraged economic development in hopes of providing employment to its residents as well as building a tax base. Maine had to develop policies that created a more inviting atmosphere for businesses to justify investing in the state. When businesses invest, they create infrastructure and hire people, thereby increasing incomes and profits and creating a tax base. In the 1800s, Maine was, like today, mostly forested. The task that the state faced was how to utilize these resources to grow the economy.

Lumber for housing was one of the first products to come from the forest. Maine was so successful in the lumber industry that in the late 1800s, Bangor, which is on the banks of the Penobscot River approximately 70 miles south of Millinocket, was the lumber capital of the world. Another use for trees was paper. Maine's vast river network was an ideal highway to get the trees from the forest to the sawmills and paper mills for processing.

Paper mills tend to be much larger than sawmills and, therefore, require a much larger capital investment. In order for companies to justify significant capital improvements, they needed to procure long-term access to trees (fiber) for the production of paper. This meant that many of the state's paper companies purchased large tracts of land for the sole purpose of having their own working forests (See figure one in appendix A for GNP's 1987 land holdings).

Companies, however, didn't want to pay taxes on the full value of the land, and so the paper industry took full advantage of the Wild Lands Tax (WLT). The WLT was a tax break on land in unorganized territories that was left as a working forest—a precursor to the Tree Growth Tax (TGT), which emerged in 1972. The WLT made it financially feasible for paper companies to control huge amounts of land, because the tax burden on landowners would be only pennies on the dollar. One of the main differences between the Wild Lands Tax and the Tree Growth Tax is that the WLT was a tax break on working forestland in unorganized territories only, whereas the TGT applies to all forested land regardless of location. In other words, WLT taxed forestland within a town or city based upon "best use," and TGT taxes it based on "current use." A retired Great Northern executive stated that the real reason for the TGT was to discourage land development.

One old article reported that paper companies controlled 52 percent of Maine's land and timber while paying only 8 percent of wages in Maine by the 1970s. The long-term effects of the Wild Lands and Tree Growth tax laws would prove detrimental to small communities, because it was in the interest of paper companies to own a working forest and not to pursue other forms of economic development or to fully diversify their investments. In the case of Millinocket, the town's original boundaries were small because the company didn't want to have to pay full taxes on forested land within the town. Some current municipal leaders claim that economic diversification would have been more likely had the town's boundaries been larger early in the town's history.

Unlike many of today's politicians, Maine lawmakers in the 1800s realized that in order to maintain and improve the state's infrastructure for the benefit of its residents, they had to encourage economic development. Accordingly, some companies sought to dam the rivers and sell hydroelectric power to the densely populated cities of southern New England. Maine quickly and wisely put a stop to this practice. Maine's governor knew that small rural communities in the state would be at a disadvantage if they had to compete with cities like Boston for electric power.

Consequently, before embarking on any building projects, companies were obliged to prove that their dams would provide an economic benefit to Maine's residents. This policy quite naturally resulted in the construction of factories, sawmills, tanning mills, textile mills, and similar industries next to any new hydropower projects. By leveraging its resources (allowing more productive uses for environmental assets), Maine developed a diverse manufacturing base and supported its communities with a broader tax base.

One of the most successful examples of these policies was the formation of Millinocket, or "The Magic City," in 1901. The nickname came about as people saw the miraculous transformation from wilderness to small city with a major factory in just a couple of years. The settlement actually dates to the 1830s, when Thomas Fowler and his family moved their farm to what is now the site of the former Great Northern Paper Company. Before this, the nearest settlement was in Medway, where the East Branch and the West Branch of the Penobscot River meet. The industries of the day were raw timber, hemlock bark (which was collected in vats for tanneries), and furs. The Penobscot River was the highway that allowed supplies to move north to Medway and raw materials to move south.

The extension of rail service from Old Town to Houlton in December 1893 helped lay the groundwork for Millinocket. It also allowed for the development of Norcross, a small whistle-stop on North Twin Lake, a few miles outside the Magic City. Norcross soon became a popular destination for sports enthusiasts and campers seeking passage to the great West Branch of the Penobscot River. Supply stores could outfit enthusiasts with all the necessary supplies; Norcross even had a small moccasin factory that employed eight to ten men.

This type of nature-based tourism, strikingly similar to what we are "inventing" today, is all fine and good, but it takes far more economic diversification to sustain and grow a thriving and healthy community.

The Vision of a Big Mill

The area where Millinocket Stream and the West Branch of the Penobscot River converge was, and still is, the most perfect spot in the world to build and operate a paper mill. The area that surrounds the location of the Millinocket mill is known as the Katahdin Region, and it remains part of the largest contiguous forest east of the Mississippi. The Katahdin Region comprises several million acres of prime-forest land with lakes and tributaries that form the Penobscot River, which was used as a highway to transport pulp wood to the mill (See figure two in appendix A). It took several bright, imaginative, and courageous men—with a team of bold financial backers, coupled with a state that was truly interested in the welfare of its residents—to motivate hundreds of hardworking craftsmen to build a paper mill that would eventually achieve worldwide fame.

By the late 1800s, much of the Katahdin area had already been surveyed and explored. Lumberjacks had long worked in this area. Floating long logs down the river during the spring rush was dangerous work, and many men went to an early grave. Charles W. Mullen, a young man from Bangor, had lumbered in this area and was familiar with the lakes and tributaries of the mighty West Branch. He was a graduate of the University of Maine with a degree in civil engineering. Mullen knew that with the addition of the Bangor and Aroostook Railroad in 1883 (which ran from Brownville through the Katahdin area, crossing Millinocket Stream on to Houlton), the area had tremendous potential. He conceived a plan to harness the river's power for the purpose of industry.

Mullen approached Garrett Schenck, the general manager and part owner of the Rumford Falls Paper Company, to entice him to build a paper mill on this section of the Penobscot. A man of tremendous vision and ambition, Schenck quickly saw the potential of Mullen's plan and began the process of starting a new mill. He sought the necessary financial backing, which enabled him to secure the necessary land rights. Schenck then enlisted Hardy Ferguson to render plans and direct the construction of a mighty mill along Millinocket Stream.

Schenck reportedly resigned his position in August of 1898. Around this time, Mullen and a group of investors, primarily from the Bangor area, formed the Northern Development Company and tried to secure land rights and financial backing for the water-power project. Being able to install dams on the river had two very important benefits for the future mill. One, the river could be harnessed for the generation of inexpensive electricity and two, it provided an efficient way to transport the pulp wood to the mill.

Two important developments happened by the spring of 1899. First, Schenck and his associates formed a new industrial company called Great Northern Paper. Second, Schenck and some large Wall Street investors replaced some of the Bangor investors on the board of the Northern Development Corporation. Finally, on May 2, 1899, the construction of the "Big Mill" began. As the *Bangor Daily News* reported, "Never has there been a piece of engineering like it in the State" (Laverty).

Amazingly, this project went from concept to construction in less than a year. Financial backing had been arranged to construct what would eventually become the world's largest paper mill under one roof. There was no town in which to locate this marvel of engineering, there were no dams in place to harness the power, there were no roads, and there was no workforce. It was located in the middle of a forest. Everything had to be brought in and built. The mill made the town; it lured the workers to it. As they were constructing the mill, carpenters scrambled to build shelters for the workers. By June, five hundred men were reported to have been working in the Magic City, and in a couple of months, that number doubled. Most of the laborers had to brave a bitter Maine winter by spending their first year in tents and makeshift shacks on the hill behind the mill (later named shack hill).

Many of the laborers were brought in from other countries. Workers came from Canada, Italy, and Eastern Europe. Some were hired by people that the company contracted to enlist workers. The company even had an employment office in Bangor, the nearest major city, seventy miles to the south.

On November 1, 1900, just eighteen months after construction had begun, Schenck prepared the first log to be sent to the grinder room to start the process for the first sheet of paper. By November 9, the first roll of newsprint was made on the Number Seven paper machine. In the early years, paper production was about two hundred fifty tons of newsprint per day and seventy-five thousand tons per year.

This project didn't simply involve building a factory with two paper machines. It involved building Stone Dam, which redirected Quakish Lake down a newly built canal. From here, the entire West Branch of the Penobscot was directed into the newly created Ferguson Pond and then through a series of seven penstocks, which enabled the West Branch to flow through the new mill (four thousand cubic feet per second can flow through the mill). The strategic location of the mill site harnessed an approximate one-hundred-ten foot drop in elevation in the reengineered river. GNP was able to harness substantial energy from the water (Fish). The water turned grinding stones, which ground the logs into fiber, and turbines that made electricity (the power generation from the grinding room will be discussed in chapter two). During this same time, Great Northern Paper Company (GNP) also began laying out the town, making streets, and starting a water company (see figure three in appendix A for a pre-1980 view of the Millinocket Mill).

For a company to accomplish any one of these tasks in less than two years was something to brag about, but to do all of them simultaneously simply boggles the mind. In today's litigious society, one couldn't even get the necessary permits in the same length of time. The events of 1899–1900, which led to the formation of the Magic City in 1901, could never again happen in the state of Maine.

Schenck and his investors undertook a massive project in a state that already had about fifteen major paper mills (Laverty). Retired Great Northern production manager Tom Griffin described Schenck and his investors as being "men of great vision—risk takers." Griffin, who spent years working in Great Northern's engineering department, went on to say, "The engineering in those early years was brilliant and out of this world." The key for GNP's investment was the location. The West Branch, which GNP eventually harnessed for use in the production of paper, plus a two-million-acre forest, which contained the fiber needed for paper, made the Katahdin region the perfect location.

Schenck and his investors arrived at the perfect time, with the perfect idea, and at the perfect location. More importantly, they were in a state that didn't get in the way and that actually encouraged them.

Working Together

GNP became the most munificent benefactor that any community could have. It designed the Magic City and paid to have the streets laid out. Millinocket was incorporated in 1901, and for the first one hundred years, the mill and the town were synonymous.

The beauty of making your own town is that you don't have any handicaps that you might encounter in the layout of an existing town. Nor do you have to deal with any of the "not in my backyard" crowd. GNP brought people into a community that it had built. Were it not for Great Northern, the community wouldn't have existed. In fact, for the first fifty years or so, if anyone spoke ill of GNP, those were considered fighting words.

By 1906, GNP continued its growth by starting another mill with four machines just a few miles to the east in what was to become East Millinocket (See figure four in Appendix A for a pre-1980s view of the East Millinocket Mill). This project involved a dam at the site of the new mill to take advantage of a twenty-five-foot drop in the river. It also involved another dam (Dolby Dam) just one mile upstream. This dam was constructed to convert the water power to electricity. Grinding stones were installed to grind wood and a concrete sluice was used to transport pulp to the new mill (the grinding stones and sluice were removed by the 1950s). The pond was said to be able to store one hundred thousand cords of wood. (We must remember that there were no log trucks; GNP also devised an ingenious system of log sluices that transported logs into and around the Millinocket mill for processing at either location.)

Despite the formation of another completely new town, GNP didn't neglect the Magic City. It was directing the construction of new streets and a water and sewer system. Through its actions in the laying out of lots, it created a de facto zoning board by separating much of the residential and commercial areas. It also hired the town's first deputy sheriff. By 1900, there were four churches and the population had exploded to two thousand people.

Great Northern Paper Company employed tremendous foresight. The Katahdin-Three (Millinocket, East Millinocket, and Medway) wisely facilitated this behavior. GNP appeared to be able to get whatever it wanted, and because everyone in the town knew where his or her bread was buttered, residents didn't dare oppose any of the mill's plans. The towns' job was to provide a quality education and a safe environment for families to live and businesses to operate. This mill's job was to invest in its business and provide employment for future generations.

Schenck and his investors did something that many modern Western businesses fail to do: they continually reinvested in their business. The continued reinvestment in expanded capacity, cost reductions, and increased quality was a strategic element of GNP's long-term success (Griffin). Aside from the initial construction in 1899 and the construction of the "East" operations in 1906, they made other major expansions—in 1914 and 1916—adding the Number Nine and Number Ten paper machines. They built several dams on the river, primarily to manage water for log drives, but eventually they installed hydroelectric generating facilities, which would become the largest privately owned system of its kind in the country. GNP's hydro system provided a highway to transport the trees that were cut from the company's forest. The hydro system eventually totaled six power-generating facilities (with a capacity of approximately 130 megawatts of electricity), to which the company added some fourteen storage dams, which regulated water levels to maximize water usage relative to power generation, paper production, and log transport.

During the 1920s, GNP continued to develop its business, but it also helped its towns with so many things. When Millinocket needed a fire truck, GNP gave it one. It was longer than the town's existing fire station, so the mill paid to have the station enlarged. Whenever either town needed anything, GNP was always the first and largest contributor. For its immeasurable generosity, GNP earned the unwavering loyalty of the community and of its employees.

I remember my grandfather talking about what the town was like in the early 1930s. The country was in the throes of the Great Depression, but the Magic City faired far better than most. He said that senior employees reduced their hours so that younger employees could work enough to support their families. The mill didn't run seven days a week until later years.

After World War II, when the US economy was the only industrialized economy left intact, demand for paper increased. GNP added the McKay Station, a hydroelectric generating facility, to Ripogenus (Rip) Dam. This became its largest power-generating facility. (It is interesting to note that the Class 5 rapids that white-water rafters enjoy as part of their "back to basics" nature-based tourism are purely the result of this hydroelectric facility.) According to a retired GNP power systems manager, the natural late-summer rate of water flow from Ripogenus is less than five hundred cubic feet per second. The current owner of GNP's hydro system is Great Lakes Hydro America (GLHA). GLHA is a subsidiary of Brookfield Renewable Resources. It releases between 1800 – 3200 cubic feet per second from Rip Dam during the same period. The importance of GNP's hydro system cannot be overstated. Old-timers used to say that one inch of rain was worth over one million dollars to GNP. A retired chief power dispatcher told me that one inch of water on GNP's hydro system amounted to 4.2 billion cubic feet of water. Given the soaring price of a barrel of oil, the value of one inch of rain must be considerably higher today.

In the 1950s, GNP installed two new paper machines (5 & 6) in East Millinocket. These machines were among the largest and fastest in the world. To help feed these machines a new modern grinding room was also installed. In East Millinocket and later in Millinocket, a first in the paper industry, high-pressure steam system was installed (1250psi). Steam heat is necessary to dry the paper after it is made and in some instances it is used to turn turbines on the machines. High-pressure steam is very expensive to install, but it is very efficient because it can be run through turbines to make electricity. The exhaust steam from the turbines is then used to dry the paper. This cools or condenses the steam so that it can return back to the boiler. In most power plants, after the steam turns the turbines, the exhaust steam is wasted by cooling it in a condenser using river water (Johnson).

About the same time that GNP added the McKay Station, Millinocket was adding a new housing development. GNP laid out the lots, made the streets, and ran the water and sewer lines. It sold the lots for just a few hundred dollars. GNP provided the lot, dug the hole for the foundation, and provided a mason to help set the forms or start laying the blocks for the foundation. It would also lend concrete-mixing machines and other tools required for the construction. Friends would get together and pour the concrete for one friend's house, and then a day or two later they would go to the others and do the same. Most of the new homeowners had full-time jobs in the mill, so they would work at the mill during the day and then work well into the night on their or their friends' houses.

The town was so united and of one mind that in the late 1940s and early 1950s, when it was apparent that the current medical facilities were inadequate, a group of people got together to raise funds for a larger hospital, which the community could control. Fund-raising for the new hospital started within the mill. Discussions with some of the unions led to an agreement for workers to contribute to the project. All of the mill workers donated a week's wages.

GNP agreed to donate $200,000 to the cause. By this time, other local residents and businesspeople were eagerly donating funds as well. In total, their efforts raised over $800,000. They didn't wait around for grants from the government, but instead they took the bull by the horns and did it themselves. (They did acquire a $10,000 grant from the state, money that was originally from a federal program. But this money was to be used exclusively for training.) (Laverty).

So the community built a modern hospital with state-of-the-art equipment that would be hard to find in any other community of this size. And it did all that without looking to the government for a handout.

Prosperity for All

The Magic City enjoyed an expansion that almost rivaled its inception fifty years earlier. GNP was constantly reinvesting in its business, and the town encouraged the company every step of the way. Millinocket's image seemed to peak in the 1950s and 1960s, when coach George Wentworth and his boys dominated boys' high school basketball. The Stearns Minutemen (Millinocket kids went to Stearns schools) regularly defeated much larger schools in the state. The height of the Minutemen's success was in 1963, when the boys from this small mill town won the New England Championships. That championship remains one of the town's most talked-about events of the last half-century.

The 1963 championship team was emblematic of the Katahdin-Three. From small, humble beginnings, the towns emerged as an economic and political powerhouse in the state. The employment rolls swelled as baby boomers came of age, and their first stop was the mill office. Recent high school graduates would "follow the window," i.e., they would go to the personnel office daily or weekly to see if there were any temporary jobs that day. After following the window for a period of time, most temporary workers would receive a permanent-worker card. Entry-level wages in the mill were so much higher than wages for equivalent work outside the mill that new hires could afford new Pontiac GTOs and Chevelles; sometimes the eager owners were so young they had to have their parents sign the purchase paperwork for the cars.

One of the perks of living in the Katahdin region is certainly the beauty of the area and the nature of its people. For those who were lucky enough to have worked at GNP in those years, the wages were a significant additional benefit. The company paid its workers twice what other local businesses could afford to pay the common laborer. The fabulous wages and benefits made it extremely difficult for small businesses in the area to attract and retain quality help. Employees at small businesses would often work just a short time in order to gain experience, and then they'd put their names in at the mill. When the mill called, they almost always went.

Working in the mill was almost a birthright. Generations of families made a good living working for GNP. School kids bragged about their dads working at the mill. They even bragged about whose dad was the best papermaker. The pride associated with working in this community, especially for GNP, was immeasurable. It seemed that nothing could slow GNP or the Magic City.

Part of the reason for GNP's continued success was its commitment to making a quality product. This was derived in great part by the engineering and research (E&R) department, which got a new state-of-the-art facility in the early 1960s. The E&R department even had a small pilot press and printing press that tested the paper and fibers for printability before new grades went to market. GNP was also noted for its great apprentice program, which always provided a pool of well-trained employees. (As a side note, a former mill manager noted that the E&R building was filled with trained technicians, engineers, and PhDs, which provided cultural diversity to the town and schools.)

The E&R department proved to be a strategic and wise decision. In 1969, before the 1972 amendments to the Clean Water Act, it fixed three problems with one solution. For years, GNP like most other companies, dumped chemicals and unused pulp fiber into the river. The quality of the river water deteriorated to the point where it started to cause quality issues in East Millinocket mill. Engineering developed and installed a MGO boiler that not only burned the "black liquor" (chemicals and pulp from the sulfite pulping process) but it also recovered the chemicals so that they could be reused. It cleaned up the river, solved the production problems in East Millinocket, and it significantly increased the efficiency of the system by generating enough high-pressure steam to not only supply the sulfite mill, but it was also used to generate electricity.

The town and mill continued to grow into the 1970s. A new Stearns High School was constructed. The housing development that the company started in the 1950s continued to expand, and the company added another trailer park to help relieve the housing shortage. McDonald's came to town, and a large shopping center moved in across the street. Business lots were in such high demand that buyers had to build on their new land within a certain period of time or else see their lots reclaimed by GNP. In one instance, GNP sold a lot to a new-car dealer and told him he had five years to have a permanent building on it or the lot would be repossessed. The dealer had the lot cleared and filled and had a portable sales office erected, but despite that, at the start of the fifth year, he got a call from the company reminding him of the terms of the sale (which called for a *permanent* building).

This illustrates the fact that the Magic City was a well-managed community. Most activities related to economic development had to have GNP's blessing. If someone wanted to locate a business in Millinocket and that person didn't have GNP's approval, it usually didn't happen. The town government had no inclination to challenge the will of the company that was its benefactor, which paid over 70 percent of the taxes and often gave gifts to the town (such as fire trucks) and funded beautification projects (such as the concrete gazebo with a copper roof in the town park).

The Magic City's unique situation made big-government "help" unnecessary. The town never had any need for government help; it had Great Northern, which made sure that the community had whatever it needed. If there was something missing, the company would find a way to fill the void. Some politicians are threatened by communities and organizations that do not need government—because that independence diminishes the influence the government has over those communities and organizations.

Furthermore, politicians frequently tell us that if the United States engages in any form of protectionism, it will devastate the economy. A form of protectionism extended beyond GNP's mighty hand. The town had a bank, the Millinocket Trust Company, and it had a local sawmill. For many years, if an individual wanted to get a loan to build a house, he or she had to own a lot with the foundation already in and the first floor installed (without walls). The bank would use this as collateral for the loan. The protectionism worked thusly: the owner of the sawmill was on the board of trustees of the bank, and if someone wanted a loan from the bank to build a house, that person had to purchase lumber from the owner of the local sawmill. The system was not perfect, but it worked.

In 1970, Great Northern Paper Company merged with Nekoosa-Edwards Paper Company of Wisconsin and became Great Northern Nekoosa. This made Great Northern a much larger company, which was listed among the *Fortune* 500, with mills both in Wisconsin and down South. GNP had already expanded into the south by 1962. The mill was in Cedar Springs, Georgia and was called Great Southern. GNN eventually ended up with several other southern mills, including state-of-the-art facilities in Leaf River, Mississippi and Ashdown, Arkansas.

During this same period, the company constructed a private road dubbed the "Golden Road." This road stretches from the mill's back door in the Magic City through the woods and out to Quebec. The Golden Road enabled the company to transport logs by truck from deep within the forest to the mill without using heavily-regulated public roads (The Golden Road will be discussed in chapter two).

The year 1973 brought yet another major capital investment. This was when the company installed its now famous Number Eleven paper machine. It was described by one former mill manager as "the last major investment in capacity in Maine." This monster machine made a roll of paper 315 inches wide and could produce more paper than several of the older machines combined. Number Eleven was capable of producing 2,700 feet of paper per minute. (After the remodeling in 2000, Number Eleven increased production to over three thousand feet per minute.) The town was growing with the company; its schools were full and the population topped out at just fewer than eight thousand in the 1970s.

During the first eighty years of their evolution, the Magic City and East Millinocket were transformed from a single-family farm dwelling in the wilderness to a small metropolis in the North Maine Woods. The Katahdin-Three's and the company's success and growth were intertwined. The region's fortune didn't rise and fall with the weather, as with farming and tourist communities. As a mother's diet affects her unborn fetus, in a single-industry town the company's business choices directly affect the health of the community.

The Katahdin-Three had so much to be thankful for. It enjoyed almost continuous growth and prosperity. Even the Great Depression couldn't dim the luster of the Magic City. Words cannot describe the wonder of this small community.

Though depressions and recessions were felt, they were not felt as they were in the rest of the country. The community always had tourists, but it didn't have to rely on them. Begging the state or federal government for money to undertake projects was unheard of. In fact, it seems that the only help that the town or Great Northern wanted from the government was to be left alone and not interfered with. When the company or the town wanted or needed something, it paid its own way with much better results than would have been realized from government assistance.

Great Northern started at a time when the state was encouraging development for the benefit of its residents. GNP invested deeply in the North Maine Woods and became the state's largest landholder and a powerful political force. It fulfilled its obligations to the residents of Maine and especially the residents of the Katahdin-Three. Perhaps this was GNP's greatest strength. After all, when a company asks the state for permission to build a dam or make a road, how much credibility would it have if it had never fulfilled previous promises?

The company made continuous capital investments that resulted in a thriving business model. When it made money, it shared its riches with the employees in the form of wages and benefits. GNP also shared its wealth with the town in many ways, the least of which was paying over 70 percent of the community's taxes.

But just as the towns and mills were enjoying a level of prosperity that the company's founder could only have dreamed of, the fortunes of both were destined to change. As an early frost marks the end of summer, by the late 1970s, the winds of change were blowing, and the sun that had shone so brightly on Millinocket and East Millinocket through its nearly eighty-year summer was soon to set. The Katahdin-Three was about to enter an economic winter that would rival an ice age.

Chapter Two

Disappearing Magic

It was inconceivable to anyone in the Katahdin region in the early 1970s that in about thirty years the massive paper mill in the Magic City would be permanently shuttered. The once cash-rich company, which at one time employed over four thousand people, would be reduced to employing about three hundred in its East operation, with just one paper machine running. The Magic City, which had one of the highest—if not the highest—per capita incomes in the state, would suffer unemployment topping 30 percent. How could the fortunes of a company and a community change so quickly and so radically?

In 1986, GNP president Robert Bartlett informed workers that in 1980 GNP's paper production reached a peak of eight hundred fifty thousand tons. By 1986 paper production was estimated to decline to six hundred ninety-five thousand tons. GNP's market share had eroded from 9.7 percent in 1980 to 7.4 percent in 1985. This was during a time when total paper consumption was rising. Part of the decline was that paper imports, from a number of countries, turned paper markets into "world-wide auctions in which the high-cost mills will not survive." This problem was exacerbated by a strong US dollar relative to foreign currencies. A strong dollar makes US exports more expensive and foreign imports less expensive, simply because of the fluctuations between the currencies. In January of 1986 the first of numerous downsizings and layoffs to help reduce GNP's cost structure was announced (Bartlett). A slow two-decade economic slide ensued, but the community still hadn't reached bottom by 2008.

Some might say that God bestowed boundless blessings upon the Katahdin-Three, and when the residents didn't appreciate it, He took the blessings away. There is no doubt that the spectacular level of blessings had to have come from God, but the collapse was all man-made. Decades of insufficient capital investment (the reasons for which will be discussed in this chapter), were not recognized by the towns of Millinocket and East Millinocket, as an omen of what was to come. The owners of the mills in the 2000s were either so short of money or could not justify investing in them that crews were occasionally forced to cannibalize parts from shuttered equipment in order to keep other machines running. After the 2003 bankruptcy, the owners of the mills scrapped significant amounts of machinery. The towns hadn't made proper financial arrangements to protect the community from an eventual drop in tax revenues. As a result, the towns lost significant tax value and in some cases the mills lost equipment that had viable use.

While the Millinocket mill is closed because of one company's decision, the economic depression that the region endures is the culmination of decades of missteps and misfortune. The fallout from the self-indulgent actions of big government, big labor, and big business was a major factor in the destruction of a thriving microcosm of capitalism. When historians look at the last thirty years, they will wonder why we stood here and allowed our community to be destroyed before our very eyes.

Millinocket's Lack of Diversification

The source of the town's fall may seem obvious given its close ties to a single company. In a one-industry town, the health of the company determines the health of the community. Naturally, the quick answer is that the town's economy was too intertwined with the company. But there were extenuating circumstances that prevented the Magic City from diversifying its economy.

First of all, Millinocket and East Millinocket would not exist without GNP. Second, as retired Great Northern production manager Tom Griffin said, "Due to the remote nature and transportation costs associated with Millinocket, if wood and water are not of extreme value to your business, there is no reason to look here" (Griffin). Third, if folks had suggested the community choose a different path, they would have been run out of town, because suggesting anything that deviated from Great Northern's plan was considered blasphemous. Great Northern was so munificent a benefactor that its word was almost gospel.

Lack of Entrepreneurial Vision

One might conclude that the fate of the town was doomed from the start, not because of evil intent on the part of a corporation, but because of its overwhelming generosity toward the town for almost seventy years. This certainly doesn't fit with what we have read about corporate America in the last thirty years, but it makes perfect sense. It is like the old saying: "If you give a man a fish, you feed him for a day, but if you teach him to fish, you feed him for life." This is exactly what happened to the Magic City. Whenever the town needed anything, Great Northern was first in line to donate to the cause. The town never learned the lessons of sound and long-lasting economic development until it was too late.

Residents were not receptive to entrepreneurial visions, because GNP's actions had the same effect on the town as big government's cradle-to-grave managed care: "Why work when GNP will give us what we need?" I don't recall hearing of any efforts on Millinocket's part to diversify its economy during the heyday of Great Northern. In fact, given the town's one-hundred-year history, economic diversification is a rather new phenomenon for the Magic City.

By the time the town got serious and started economic development in the 1990s, the local economy had already started a long, painful downhill slide that would resist all efforts to reverse it. The delay to diversify was a major mistake, because any businessperson worth his or her salt will say that if a business has a customer that accounts for over 70 percent of its business, that business needs to increase its customer base as quickly as possible. And remember, for many decades, Great Northern paid over 70 percent of the taxes in the Magic City. Over the last several years, the town worked diligently on diversification, but the Magic City missed its easiest opportunity.

If success breeds success, the reverse is also true. Once a community acquires the "stink of death," businesses shun it. Businesses located in such a community don't need much of an excuse to leave. And if a business is looking to relocate, it usually does not consider moving to a community that is suffering an economic slide.

This happens in part because many large businesses consider long-term planning only as far as the next quarter. Intense pressure from Wall Street investors forces large companies to concentrate on maximizing short-term profits. Too much focus on short-term profits cripples the long-term value of businesses, because it causes a lack of capital investment. When it is no longer viable for companies to maintain operations, they are forced to close. Business closures are a symptom of economically depressed communities. Certain people are interested in these stricken communities, however, and history has shown that shysters, false prophets, and general crooks all swarm in and find a way to instill a sense of false hope in an effort to get a free handout. In the case of the Magic City, some of these charlatans were found out before they got any money, but others took the money and ran. Companies with a plan like Great Northern's original vision have become a thing of the past.

The Town's Size

We know that the Magic City was not able to diversify its economy until it was too late, but the town did try to make a strategic move in the mid-1970s that could have had significant long-term benefits. The town sought to significantly expand its border to the west. The expansion would have taken in a part of the lakes created by the North Twin Dam. A similar expansion was proposed by a town councilor in 2005, but the efforts failed both times. The original footprint of the town was a mere eleven square miles and offered little in the way of economic expansion. The town later sought this expansion in an effort to create opportunities.

The North Twin Dam would most likely have fallen within this annexation, as well as many camps or seasonal cottages. The revenue from this expansion would have provided the town with much-needed money; in recent years, conditions within the paper industry had forced the town to lower Great Northern's tax burden from over 70 percent of the town's budget to about 45 percent. A lower tax burden was intended to aid the company in maintaining profitability and thus future investment. This expansion would also have allowed camp owners to deal with the town instead of Maine's infamous Land Use Regulation Commission

(Department of Environmental Protection regulations would still have to be followed). LURC, as it is known, has become a tremendous obstacle to economic development in Maine's unorganized territories.

LURC was formed in 1971 as an administrative agency with authority to oversee planning and zoning in the unorganized townships. Its jurisdiction encompasses over ten million of Maine's twenty-one million acres. In 2011, I was in a closed-door meeting with Maine's Governor, Paul LePage, and thirty to forty other businesspeople, and when the topic of LURC arose, several of the prominent businesspeople said LURC was their biggest fear. Business leaders cite a potentially long, slow, and expensive permitting process for many forms of development as a hindrance to expansion.

The tragedy of the first failed North Twin expansion is that it wasn't Great Northern that blocked the annexation but rather the local residents, who voted against it because they didn't want property taxes on their camps to rise. When the camps are in an unorganized territory, the taxes are paid to the State of Maine; when they fall within a community, the owners have to pay the town's rate, which is often higher. Given the area's shrinking tax base, the extra revenue from the tax on camp lots would allow the community a level of economic diversification. A broader tax base helps to shield the community from disaster when the valuation on its largest taxpayer's property is reduced.

The camp lots remained under the control of Great Northern and/ or its successors. But in 2012, Katahdin Timberlands announced that it was going to sell the camp lots. The lots, which leased for fifty dollars in the 1970s, leased for $2,000–$3,000 by 2013. Also, one of the perks of being a Great Northern retiree was that retirees were entitled to one free camp lease. This practice ended around 2006.

The growing power of LURC surely hampered a potentially limitless economic asset for the communities. Furthermore, with increased development, the town would have had the benefit of significantly higher tax revenues, which would potentially reduce the impact of the lower valuation of GNP's former Millinocket mill.

Town Rivalries

The Katahdin-Three—Millinocket, East Millinocket, and Medway—made a mistake that rendered the communities even less attractive than other northern Maine communities. The towns' mistake was in how each protected big-government values. It is hard to imagine small towns having big-government values, but they do. Each community, in an effort to protect its unique identity, chose to remain almost completely autonomous in providing most services to its respective residents. As a result, the communities have greatly underutilized economies of scale. Higher taxes and an unfortunate rivalry between the communities have stifled economic growth. The towns failed to realize that Millinocket, East Millinocket, and Medway are one community separated by three names.

In 2005, the Millinocket Area Growth and Investment Council (MAGIC) commissioned a study by the University of Maine for the purpose of attracting a retailer for a vacant fifty-thousand-square-foot building. One of the observations in the study was that from 1980 to 2005, Millinocket and the town of Lincoln had traded places in terms of retail sales. Millinocket went from having a net influx of three to four million dollars in general-merchandise sales to having a loss of three million dollars in general-merchandise sales. Stated differently, people from outlying areas used to shop in Millinocket, and now they and the local residents shop outside Millinocket.

Lincoln is thirty-five miles south of Millinocket and has a small paper mill that has had some of the same economic problems as Millinocket's. The town of Lincoln, however, is run more efficiently and has become a more attractive place to locate a business. That efficiency enables Lincoln to provide a local property tax rate of $20.12, versus Millinocket's $25.60 for the 2012 tax year. Lincoln's land area is 76.8 square miles, compared with Millinocket's 18.3. Lincoln's population is larger, but its municipal and school budgets are lower. Millinocket's 2010 municipal budget was over $6 million, whereas Lincoln's 2011 municipal budget was just over $5 million. Millinocket's 2010 school budget was just over $5 million, compared with Lincoln's $3.7 million. One example of Lincoln's efforts to seek out economic efficiencies is its participation in a regional school unit (RSU). RSUs are formed when several neighboring communities send their students to one school to take advantage of economies of scale or efficiencies that come from eliminating unneeded duplication of services provided by nearby communities.

Part of the Katahdin Region's inability to attract a general-merchandise retailer is attributable to the lack of cooperation between the towns and the resulting lack of local-government efficiency. Such conditions lead to unstable tax rates. With better cooperation between the surrounding communities, Millinocket, East Millinocket, and Medway would be able to take advantage of economies of scale and provide a lower and more stable tax rate that is less dependent upon the mills. Low stable tax rates are one of the keys to attracting entrepreneurs to a community.

School consolidation between Millinocket, East Millinocket, and Medway was proposed in the early 1990s and again in 2009. Across all three towns, 438 residents were in favor of the consolidation and 412 were against it, but because of where those 438 were distributed, only one of the communities voted in favor, and therefore consolidation never happened. Despite a 2002 study that showed a potential savings of $450,000 if Stearns High School and Schenck High School were merged, some of the leaders in the communities denounced the merger and protected their own town's identity over improving the overall economic health of the region. It seems counterintuitive, but even small-town governments have the desire to manipulate their residents in order to preserve themselves over the interests of the community.

All three of the towns, at one time or another, have thwarted sharing or have caused animosity among the communities. Regardless of how the votes go or what was done in the past, each of the towns needs to respect the others' sovereignty. Millinocket, East Millinocket, and Medway each have to receive tangible benefits from consolidation. Until there is mutual respect and shared benefits, all three of the towns will continue to languish in a malaise.

A retired Millinocket School Board member told me that the estimated savings in the early 1990s was one million dollars a year. Here again, each community chose itself and its bureaucracy over the economy of the region. If $1 million per year was invested at 6 percent for twenty years, it would total $38.9 million. Had the communities looked out for the health of the region in 1990 and merged all three towns into one large town or administrative structure, an additional $1 million in potential savings should have been realized. If $2 million a year had been invested at 6 percent, it would total $77.9 million. The time-value calculations may be the only way to illustrate the power and positive effect of the potential savings from seeking economies of scale.

In the early 1990s, the mills were paying approximately 70 percent of Millinocket's budgets. (Millinocket's town manager, Eugene Conologue, told me that for 2012, Cate Street Capital would be paying approximately 45 percent of the town's budget.) Seventy percent of $2 million is $1.4 million. If simply added over twenty years, that totals $28 million. Granted, the mill's proportion of tax liabilities to the towns has declined in recent years due to tax abatements and other incentives, but in the 1990s an extra $1.4 million profit would have looked good to the company.

If the communities were serious about economic development, a complete merger of the three towns would occur. Such a merger would provide significant savings as a result of reduced duplication of services. The towns have successfully combined or provided mutual support on some services, but there is no need for three separate town offices, transfer stations, fire departments, police departments, and public works departments. City mergers can be controversial, because the promised savings do not always materialize. In the case of the Katahdin-Three, a merger would not and should not occur unless it provided significant cost savings to all the taxpayers. A remarketing of the combined community could potentially make the region a small service hub.

A merger among five communities created the city of Miramichi in northern New Brunswick, Canada, in 1995. Since the merger, its retail offerings have expanded. Several new restaurants, retail stores, and automobile dealerships have opened. Miramichi had a paper mill close in September of 2007, but, unlike Millinocket, Miramichi chose to seek efficiencies before its mill closed and it tried something new in order to grow its economy. While Miramichi's economy has struggled, there is a sense of better days ahead. New businesses are opening their doors, and that is the key to economic prosperity.

The overwhelming generosity of Great Northern, combined with government subsidies in the aftermath of the GNP bankruptcy, caused Millinocket to lose the atmosphere that embraced entrepreneurs. There was no need for residents in the community to develop new solutions, because there was always GNP or the government to come to their rescue. The problem is, there are no more rescues. Lasting economic growth comes from entrepreneurs, not from government spending. Millinocket and East Millinocket were created out of an entrepreneurial spirit, and until that spirit returns, the region will continue to languish with an anemic economy.

The Company's Role

Great Northern Paper Company and its successors didn't maliciously set out to destroy the Katahdin-Three's economy, but each successive owner seemed to have an increasing aura of self-indulgence, which played a part in the community's decline. GNP built the town, and the town's success was a source of pride for the company for decades.

However, each time the company was merged with another, taken over, or sold to another company, the owners became increasingly removed from the community. This increased distance allowed the new owners to consider only the company's needs. Former president Bill Clinton alluded to this trend in a 2011 interview. He said that companies in the past would weigh the needs of the shareholders, employees, and the communities in which they were located when making decisions. Now, he said, they consider only the needs of the shareholders. The former president's comments are an oversimplification of the problem, but they help illustrate a disturbing and destructive trend in America.

In Millinocket's case, the company didn't have an overnight transformation from benefactor to Grinch. Some of the company's behavior was necessary for its initial success, but as time evolved, some of these actions not only harmed the community but harmed the company as well.

Local Land Control

One area in which the company was very controlling was with its land. GNP needed absolute control over all of its land because the company knew that its long-term plan required trees for the production of paper, and it couldn't afford to have precious trees used for any purpose other than paper production. Because it controlled all the land, this enabled the company to control economic development. As stated earlier, it wasn't necessary for the town to actively engage in economic development, because GNP provided such a spectacular level of prosperity.

There are several local stories in which the company allegedly discouraged economic development. Old-timers often maintain that Great Northern didn't want to have to compete for labor with any other companies. In terms of wages, GNP wouldn't have had to compete, as it paid the highest wages in the state. What was worrisome was that another company in a different industry might offer lower wages but provide a much more hospitable working environment. And employees might indeed take a cut in pay in return for a better quality of life.

There is no convincing evidence that GNP and its successors thwarted economic diversification in the post-World War II era. The reality of the situation is that GNP was paying the highest wages in the state, it controlled virtually all of the natural resources in the area, and Millinocket had near-zero unemployment and domicile vacancy. GNP's retired town site manager, Frederic Morrison, said that in all his years in the department, he never had a company approach GNP about locating a factory in the Katahdin region.

The company did, however, have policies that prevented land speculators from buying lots in the town. New house and business lots became available only when most of the existing inventory of lots had been sold. As mentioned earlier, the terms of sale would often include a specified time frame to build and the value of the proposed project; the latter was intended to prevent an undesirable shack city (Morrison).

GNP also had a habit of creating small house and business lots. It wasn't a frequent occurrence, but if someone wanted a multi-acre house lot, GNP simply said it didn't have any available for sale (Morrison). It wasn't until the 1970s, under Morrison, that house lots got to a more desirable size, and the area did not have an industrial park until the 1980s, when the company provided fifty thousand dollars and instructed its town site manager, Jim Carson, to create an industrial park (Carson). The industrial park had little success. By the time it opened, the company was downsizing dramatically, and a few years later, the country had a major recession. In addition to those factors, northern Maine in general did not attract investment dollars, because of burdensome state regulations, which will be discussed in the "The State's Role" section of this chapter.

Even though GNP didn't overtly thwart investment, had it been more liberal in selling some of the land it owned in the first fifty or sixty years of the town's existence, and had it created the industrial park decades earlier, Millinocket and neighboring towns surely would have developed beyond the current state. Tight controls over the availability of lots did appear to slow the cadence of the development of smaller businesses in the community. The businessman who purchased a lot in the late 1950s with a five-year promise to build on the site had actually been looking for a suitable lot in Millinocket for almost ten years before he found one that allowed enough space for growth.

GNP's monopoly over the land may have been a factor that prevented Millinocket from diversifying the economy in the town's early years. However, communications that I had with former GNP vice president, Jim Giffune, and Marcia McKeague, president of Katahdin Timberlands LLC, the current owners of the land, indicate that the availability of land for development has not been an issue for Millinocket's economic diversification in recent years. In recent decades, northern Maine has lagged behind the nation in economic development, and there has been little interest in obtaining land for development in Millinocket. Many experts cite Maine's regulatory environment as being the chief obstacle to development.

The Merger

Some in the Magic City cite the 1970 merger with Nekoosa-Edwards Paper, thus forming Great Northern Nekoosa (GNN), as the beginning of the end. They feel that because it was no longer just the two Maine mills, there was a marked change in the amount of capital investment in the Maine mills. In 1962, Great Northern made an investment in a mill in Cedar Springs Georgia, but the merger with Nekoosa seemed to exacerbate the change in capital outlays. This eventually led to the lack of competitiveness and profitability for these mills. Griffin said that GNP went from being a small company to a major corporation overnight. He added that larger corporations have a tendency, due to their size, to impose "one size fits all" solutions that lack the personal attention and knowledge of the employees and communities that smaller companies have. These personal touches help to create a sense of loyalty to the company (Griffin).

There was in fact a marked change in the amount of capital investment. One retired manager said, "The Nekoosa people were much better at selling their plans than we were. We were simply outsold." Many of the retired employees say that the mills of the Great Southern, another division of GNN, were built with profits from the Maine mills. True again, but the GNN years were not without investment. The legendary Number Eleven paper machine, one of just three in the world like it, was installed under GNN's watch. Retired GNP vice president Jim Giffune describes it as one of the last major investments in paper-production capacity in Maine. GNN also rebuilt two machines in the East operation in the mid-1980s to better develop quality newsprint in order to compete with Canadian companies.

The Need for Modernization and Full-Fiber Utilization

Looking back, one can see the company made some strategic mistakes. It delayed for decades the implementation of wider, faster, and less labor-intensive machines. In *Timber!: The Fall of Maine's Paper Giant*, Paul McCann mentioned that a GNP president in the 1940s had scrapped plans to install new wider machines. It wasn't until the 1950s that the new-style machines were installed in the East Millinocket operation. He said that the Canadians started using new machines in the late 1920s and 1930s. My grandfather worked on the big machines in Quebec and New

Brunswick, Canada. Almost twenty years later, he was able to work on the big machines when they were installed in the GNP mills.

The company must have had a good reason to stick with the 1900s vintage machines as long as it did, but delaying more cost-effective forms of production placed GNP at a competitive disadvantage. The company continued to improve the quality of the paper, and added an on machine coater to Number Ten paper machine (an off-machine coater for Number Seven and Eight) to make more profitable shiny grades of paper, but the paper machines were still narrow, slow, and labor-intensive. New machines are wider and faster and can produce more tons of paper with fewer people.

Despite less efficient machines, GNN's Maine mills remained a powerhouse in the paper industry into the 1970s and 1980s. The company's two million acres of forest and its hydroelectric system provided such a competitive advantage that it enabled the company to shift necessary capital improvements to other locations. Much of the company's investments were made in GNN's Ashdown and Leaf River mills in southern United States.

One of the company's goals was always full-fiber utilization. In other words, it wanted to make use of all the species of wood on its land, not just the spruce and fir that were used in the papermaking process. In the 1950s, it experimented with something called "chemigroundwood" pulp. The chemigroundwood process used some of the company's abundant poplar in the pulping process. Pulping is a term used to describe the various ways logs are broken down into small fibers that can be made into paper. The company publicized the process in a trade publication with a picture of an employee transferring a roll of paper containing chemigroundwood. It was a different pulping process, but it was fraught with difficulties and was therefore abandoned.

GNN did attempt a measure of diversification with the purchase of Pinkham Lumber, a sawmill in Aroostook County. The company made capital investments in the mill, but the sawmill struggled to make profits (McCann). Some familiar with the operation said that three things happened: first, the employees joined a union when GNN purchased the mill, thus raising labor costs; second, the cost of obtaining fiber or saw logs increased due to a variety of factors, including issues stemming from the state (like environmental regulations, workers' compensation, and taxes, which I cover in a later section); and third, the housing market declined.

GNN had another opportunity to diversify, and that was the opportunity to develop a plant making waferboard, or *oriented strand board* (OSB). The investment would have been only sixty million dollars, and the return on investment was very favorable. Great Northern Paper wanted the project to proceed, but its parent company GNN decided, despite having lumber operations in other divisions, not to invest in the OSB plant, because it wanted to focus on making paper (McCann).

OSB plants use poplar wood to manufacture an inexpensive plywood substitute. GNN had an ample supply of the wood. In the end, a former GNN employee helped Louisiana Pacific (LP) build a plant to make this product near Houlton, Maine, an hour north of Millinocket. The LP mill was successful and attracted a one-hundred-fifty-million-dollar modernization investment in the late 2000s (Louisiana Pacific). Former GNP executive Jim Giffune told me that full-fiber utilization was never realized by GNP in Maine. This left the region and the company dependent solely on paper.

By the 1980s, the more efficient Canadian machines were producing paper much more cheaply than GNP could produce it on the old machines. During the same time, the Millinocket mill was producing more paper than any other mill in Maine, but it also had the most employees. Even with hundreds fewer employees, modern mills could produce as much paper as the Millinocket mill (McCann). When the paper industry became a global business, the costs of running old machines in the Maine mills became a problem (Griffin). The decision to forgo modernization decades earlier sealed Millinocket's fate.

The Millinocket mill had plans, in the 1980s, for a new pressurized-groundwood pulping facility, a kraft plant, and new modern paper machines. Some of the projects were very advanced. Key management employees made trips to Europe to study modern pulping facilities and paper machines. Unfortunately for Millinocket, corporate politics (GNN not funding the projects), a hostile takeover, and state politics prevented virtually all of the investments.

The lack of a modern pulping facility was a part of the Millinocket mill's demise. In 1986, GNP president Robert Bartlett stated that "A modernization of our sulfite mill in Millinocket is absolutely essential if we are to produce pulps competitive in quality with kraft pulp carried in most of the papers we compete against" (Bartlett). Some investments were made and the quality of sulfite pulp improved significantly over the next several years, but for many of the grades of paper that the company was producing in the 2000s, sulfite pulp was still less desirable than kraft pulp.

Kraft pulping is a different process than GNN's sulfite process. As a rule, sulfite pulp (the process that GNP used) is usually less expensive to produce, but kraft usually provides a longer, stronger, and brighter fiber and thus has better printability and is more desirable. A modern kraft-pulping facility would also enable the company to use some of its other very abundant species of wood like poplar, rather than just using spruce and fir, thus getting closer to full-fiber utilization.

There are two schools of thought on the kraft pulp vs. sulfite pulp debate. The first group of experts point to the improvements to the sulfite pulping system under Bowater in the 1990s. In an effort to make the sulfite pulp emulate the characteristics of kraft pulp, new presses to kink the fibers and a hydrogen peroxide bleaching system were installed. These improvements increased the tear strength and brightness of the pulp, and therefore improved the paper. On one occasion, when a southern Bowater paper mill was temporarily shut down, some of the orders for paper were diverted to the Katahdin region mills. When the southern plant came back online, the customer wanted to continue to get its paper from the Maine mills.

The second group of experts agrees that the sulfite pulp was greatly improved by the time of the bankruptcy in 2003, but they maintain that kraft pulp was still stronger, brighter and had better printing characteristics. In the years leading up to the bankruptcy, the price of kraft pulp became more competitive with sulfite pulp. One expert familiar with the situation, said that when the mills emerged from bankruptcy, kraft pulp purchased on the open market was more economical than continuing the operation of GNP's sulfite mill. The new owner, Katahdin Paper a subsidiary of Canadian conglomerate Brascan (Brascan will be discussed later in this chapter), decided to use kraft pulp and demolished the sulfite mill.

As GNP was forced to shut down its old, slow, and labor intensive paper machines, new modern ones were not installed. Those familiar with the paper business have told me that profit comes from volume of production. They state that as production is increased, the fixed costs are spread over greater amounts of product and the total cost per ton is reduced as a result. At its peak, when all its machines were running, GNP's sulfite system produced about five hundred tons of sulfite pulp a day. This is in comparison to modern kraft mills that produce one thousand five hundred to two thousand tons a day. Former executives told me that without new fast, machines to increase output, the fixed overhead of a kraft mill that produced less than five-hundred tons a day would be too high.

Regardless of whether kraft pulp is better than the mills improved sulfite pulp, GNP's paper machines and sulfite pulping system needed upgrading. The capital investments that did occur in later years were slow in coming, and many investments that needed to be made never happened.

Great Northern Paper's parent company, Great Northern Nekoosa (GNN), took profits and diverted capital investments from the Millinocket mills and invested them in its mills in the southern United States. Several former GNP managers told me that they noticed a direct relationship between the capital needs of the southern mills and the Maine mills. They said that as the capital budgets went up in the southern mills, they went down in Millinocket. GNN's massive investments in its southern operations created state-of-the-art facilities that caught the eye of Georgia-Pacific (GP).

The Hostile Takeover

In 1989, Georgia Pacific (GP) issued a cash tender offer of three billion dollars for Great Northern Nekoosa. GNN viewed the offer as uninvited and resisted what it saw as a hostile takeover. GP sued, and in *Georgia-Pacific Corporation, et al. v. Great Northern Nekoosa Corporation, et al.*, Great Northern testified that GP intended to sell some of GNN's assets, including the Maine assets. GNN cited GP studies, which dated as far back as 1984, that indicated that GP's profits could be maximized by "improving winners and eliminating losers." The court was satisfied that GP didn't intend to sell the Maine assets, and the company was awarded injunctive relief from impediments to its twice-declined offer. The impediments were "poison pills" that GNN used to prevent the hostile takeover. Many companies have provisions in place to make them less attractive to a larger company trying to institute a hostile takeover.

Many former GNN employees questioned GNN executives' sincerity in fighting the hostile takeover. The premium that GP offered for the GNN stock provided GNN's top executives and institutional investors a significant incentive to allow the takeover. The very top executives had the potential to increase their personal wealth by several million dollars due to stock options and bonuses that resulted from the takeover.

GP didn't have the mills for long, and didn't have any time to invest in the Maine facilities. GP did, however, have time to halt a five-hundred-million-dollar expansion at the Millinocket site. GNN had partnered with MD Paper (of Germany) as an equity partner to build a mill in Millinocket that involved a new pulping process of turning logs into usable fiber for paper. According to David Roop, a retired senior market analyst for GNN, the end product was going to be a marketable coated groundwood paper. The project had advanced to the point where the equipment had been selected and environmental permitting was well advanced when GP's hostile takeover was complete. GP immediately stopped work on the project, and the planned investment never materialized (Doody).

The new mill would have been a great boost for the local economy and would have ensured the long-term viability of the Millinocket mills. A new, modern, and efficient papermaking process, in theory, allows more profits, which in turn allows continued operation and investment. The hostile takeover destroyed those plans and handicapped the future of the town.

Another New Owner

A short eighteen months after Georgia-Pacific purchased Great Northern Nekoosa, it announced that it was selling its Millinocket mills and accompanying assets to Bowater Paper Company. The town of Millinocket openly welcomed the sale, because during the hostile takeover and the ensuing trial, GNN asserted that GP had evaluated the entire corporation and had implied that the Maine assets were undesirable (*Georgia-Pacific Corporation, et al., Plaintiffs v. Great Northern Nekoosa, et al., Defendants*). Bowater was a new start for a tired community.

When Bowater, under chairman and chief executive officer A.P. Gammie, took over the Millinocket mills, it renamed the division Great Northern Paper and installed W.P. "Bob" Gregory as its president. I knew Gregory, and I believe that he and Bowater had good intentions for the Maine assets. Shortly after he came to town, he told my brother and me that he wanted a Chevrolet S10 Blazer for a company car, and he specifically told the purchasing department to "check with the locals first." That was a powerful change in attitude, because a purchasing agent once told a local dealer that the company used to shop for vehicles locally but would purchase from an out-of-town dealer if the savings was as little as fifty dollars.

Shortly after assuming ownership, Bowater built a recycling plant at the East Millinocket complex that de-inked old newspapers and prepared the fiber to be reused and added into new paper. Market conditions required the construction of the recycling plant—customers demanded that their paper have a certain percentage of recycled fiber. Bowater stepped up and built a state-of-the-art facility that helped add to the viability of the East operation for the next two decades. But Bowater struggled with the mills, and it announced a major layoff in the early 1990s. I spoke with Bob Gregory at the time, and he said in an empathetic manner, "What they don't realize is that I had to stop the bleeding."

On one occasion, Gregory alluded to past decisions by the previous owners of the mill and how they affected his ability to run Bowater/Great Northern. In a heated discussion between him and a neighbor of mine, I heard my neighbor ask why Bowater/GNP was cutting so much wood, to which Gregory promptly replied, "For the next five years, we can only cut four hundred thousand cord a year, because the previous owners overcut big time." He wouldn't say which company he had suspected of overcutting trees, but former GNN executives told me that their land had more trees on it in the 1980s than when it took ownership of it at the turn of the century.

Whoever overharvested the trees, the phenomenon illustrates an important point. The law of unintended consequences basically states that actions can have outcomes that are completely different from the desired outcome. Corporations, governments, and unions are forever making decisions only to see results that they never expected. In this case, according to a Bowater/GNP executive, a previous owner overharvested trees. The trees might have been sold, and therefore the overharvesting presumably added to revenues. But, ironically, that increase led to reduced harvesting and less revenue a short time later.

Another of Bowater's legacies was that it removed the wood grinders (which turn the pulp wood into fibers, which are then used as the main furnish in the papermaking process) and replaced them with water turbines that produce electricity. Millinocket's wood room and grinding room were labor intensive, and the added fiber of East Millinocket's recycle plant freed up enough grinding capacity in East Millinocket's mill to supply Millinocket with fiber. By eliminating the expense of labor and increasing electrical supply, Bowater's decision to remove the grinding room and use it make electricity proved a brilliant way to maximize the value of the water power generated by the West Branch (36 megawatts of electricity), which runs through the building, but the decision had lasting repercussions. A little more than ten years later, when the mills were owned by Inexcon, Maine's legislature allowed the company's hydro system to be separated and sold to a third party. The turbines located in the old Millinocket grinding room were part of that sale. From that point forward, the Millinocket mill would neither have a grinding room nor own the electricity.

When fully operational, East's grinding room could produce sufficient levels of pulp to compensate for the loss of the grinding room in Millinocket. But as time passed, the situation changed. Production workers told me that, near the end of Katahdin Paper's ownership (Katahdin Paper is the name given to the mills when they were purchased out of bankruptcy), the East Millinocket mill's grinding room was in need of repairs and as a result was no longer able to produce enough quality fiber for both mills. Quality paper with sufficient strength and printability cannot be made without quality fiber.

A more recent example of the unintended consequences of corporate decisions is the result of Inexcon's (see the Behind the Bankruptcy section) and Katahdin Paper's reduced maintenance services. The mill's former fire chief told me that executives significantly reduced the cleaning crews within the mill. It saved money in the short term, but the nature of the paper business is that it produces a lot of paper and wood dust, which is highly flammable. The result was increased incidents of fire within the plant. (The fire chief told me that while fire is more expensive than a cleaning crew, a blaze is a great cleaner.) Fires aside, reducing maintenance is just generally costly, as equipment becomes less efficient and liable to break down. Thus, the decisions of the past dictate the expenses of the future.

In the late 1990s, Bowater/GNP announced a plan to invest $150 to $200 to modernize the East Millinocket mill. At the same time, the company announced that it was looking for buyers for the Millinocket mill (Legasse). Decades of neglect had relegated the Millinocket mill to being a loser. The East complex was spared because of its recycling plant and its Number Five and Number Six paper machines, was installed in the 1950s and then upgraded in the mid-1980s. Gordon Manuel, GNN's spokesman, announced that the scheduled modernization was to be completed in early 2000.

Big business, however, got in the way of the proposed modernization. Bowater, under its chief executive officer, Arnold M. Nemirow, a former Great Northern Nekoosa executive, announced the $2.5 billion purchase of Avenor Inc., a forest-products company based in Canada. Shortly before the official vote of the Bowater shareholders, Nemirow announced that Bowater would consider selling all of its Maine assets after the pending purchase of Avenor was completed (Legasse).

Near the same time, Bowater/GNP had expressed interest in using natural gas from the Maritime Pipeline in part of its operation. The natural gas company was going to build a spur to the Magic City. At the last minute, however, Bowater backed out. The company didn't mention this to the community until it was too late to intervene. There were plans to build a natural gas power-generating facility in town as well. Unfortunately, Bowater's plans involved selling off parts of the company first and then selling the paper mill later. So the natural gas power-generation facility was instead built in Veazie, Maine.

I had a conversation with a retired Bowater employee, who said that the company pulled out because it couldn't get anyone else to sign on to use the natural gas. That made the cost of constructing the pipeline prohibitive to Bowater's plans for the mills. A short time later, Bowater sold over 1.5 million acres of forest land, and the mills in Millinocket and East Millinocket. The investment in a natural gas pipeline would have lowered the long-term energy costs of the mills, but in my analysis the costs couldn't be recovered fast enough for Bowater to warrant the investment.

This wasn't the first time alternatives to oil were discussed for the mills. After the 1973 Arab oil embargo, GNN developed a plan to wean the company off oil. The first part was to build a biomass boiler in East Millinocket that would allow 60 percent production with no oil. The second part was to convert two boilers in Millinocket to use coal (two boilers would not supply all of Millinocket's steam needs). The biomass boiler was built in East, but the eighty-million-dollar coal project, which would have potentially saved eight hundred thousand barrels of oil per year was never constructed (McCann). The company seriously considered burning coal and wood in Millinocket, but the economics of the situation at the time didn't warrant switching from oil (Johnson). A hydroelectric dam was also considered and then shelved. The dam project and its proposal in the mid-1980s will be discussed under the state section.

Behind the Bankruptcy

In the end, Bowater sold its Maine assets piece by piece to maximize shareholder value at the expense of the economy of northern Maine. Sanabe & Associates, an investment-banking boutique, developed the plan that divided the Maine assets and allowed Bowater to sell the holdings for 50 percent more than the company expected. Sanabe reported that Bowater netted four hundred fifty million dollars on the sale (Sanabe & Associates LLC). Inexcon, a small Quebec-based investment group headed by Lambert Bedard, purchased the mills, four hundred thousand acres of land, and the hydro system. Irving, a Canadian conglomerate, purchased one million acres and the old Pinkham Lumber sawmill.

Inexcon took ownership of the mills in 1999 and immediately started planning a one-hundred-million-dollar modernization of Millinocket's Number Eleven paper machine. It was discovered during the 2003 bankruptcy of Inexcon that, the day it took ownership of the Bowater/GNP mills, a transfer of seven million dollars from the Maine mills to Bedard, Inexcon's chief executive officer, made the company insolvent.

In order to raise money for the remodeling and to maintain operation of the mills, Inexcon/GNP raised fifty million dollars by selling forty thousand acres of land, and it placed another two hundred thousand acres into a conservation easement. It then convinced the Maine legislature to modify the company's hydro charter to allow it to be separated and sold to Great Lakes Group, a wholly-owned subsidiary of Brascan Corporation, a Canadian conglomerate. That provided $156.5 million, which was necessary to finish the remodel of Number Eleven paper machine (Lagasse, GNP Power Sale...). The remodeling came too late, and Inexcon simply didn't have pockets deep enough to make other necessary upgrades that would have made the mills more viable.

The value of the electricity that the hydroelectric dams produced became apparent to me when Inexcon owned the mills. For years the mills had sold excess power to the electric grid, but I was told that under Inexcon, production schedules were occasionally modified to maximize the electricity available to sell. Given market prices for paper, it was more lucrative to generate electricity than produce paper.

Former President of the Maine State Senate, Charles Pray, informed me that when the Maine Legislature originally granted water rights to GNP in the late 1800s, it tied those rights to the proposed paper mill. Therefore any effort to sell or separate the dams from the paper mills needed to be approved by the Maine Legislature. Furthermore, Pray stated that Brascan had to seek permission from the Federal Energy Regulatory Commission (FERC) to be able to sell power on to the New England power grid. In an effort to try to repair the once strategic link between the mills and the dams, LD 543 was signed into law by Governor John Baldacci, in 2010. The law gives the mills a right of first refusal on the electricity that the dams produce (Sambides Jr., 2010).

(As a side note, the estimated cost to build the proposed Big A dam, in the mid-1980s, was one-hundred-million dollars. That figure compounded at five percent annually equates to over two-hundred-million dollars by 2002. Inexcon had five hydro-electric dams plus numerous other smaller storage dams. If the construction cost for each of the hydro-electric dams in 2002 was approximately two-hundred-million dollars, then the one-hundred-and-thirty megawatt hydroelectric system's replacement cost would be approximately one billion dollars.)

In 2003, Inexcon/GNP filed for bankruptcy. People who retired when Bowater owned the mills found out that they no longer had their retirement health insurance, because Inexcon had assumed the liability when it purchased the mill. The company was completely insolvent, and both mills were forced to shut down in the middle of the winter with only a few hours notice. Tom Griffin, one of the three former GNN executives who helped negotiate the sale of the mills after the bankruptcy, said that he was very impressed with the results of the Number Eleven rebuild, but the cost of it destroyed the company. He also felt that the sale of the hydro system was the final nail in the Millinocket mill's coffin (Griffin).

A maintenance worker in the East Millinocket mill said that he and several others on his crew refused orders to stop working and leave. He told me that when his boss told him to leave the pipes without draining them, he replied, "F— You! What are you going to do? Fire me?" Another of his bosses told him, "You know what to do and you know what needs to be done." They took the extra hours necessary to drain as many essential lines and properly shutter as much of the plant as possible. Unfortunately, the funds necessary to restart the shuttered mills could have been better used by the eventual buyer for efficiency upgrades that would have improved viability.

The selfless efforts by the East crew were an important factor in getting the mill reopened as quickly as it did. In hindsight, it was a bright spot and a potential turning point in the attitudes and actions of the employees and community. Only time will tell if this shift in attitude will develop into the fighting spirit that created the town.

During the bankruptcy process, three former GNP executives—Jim Giffune, Tom Griffin, and Warren Richardson—donated their time to help find a buyer that would reopen the mills. These men were respected not only in the paper industry but also by the workers and towns. Without their efforts, it is hard to imagine what would have happened to the Millinocket and East Millinocket plants. Giffune said that trying to find a quality buyer was an almost impossible task because of Maine's unfriendly business climate. Tom Griffin said that most of the companies that they contacted had no interest in the mills, because of the reputation of Maine; the reputation, in the industry, of the Millinocket mill being old and antiquated; and the fact that the mills were separated from the massive hydro system. Maine's poor business climate not only deterred potential investors, but it was one of the reasons the Maine mills had failed to attract necessary capital investments while GNN owned them.

Life after the Bankruptcy

Brascan, which is based in Toronto, Canada, and which was renamed Brookfield Asset Management, purchased the shuttered mills in 2003. The sale to Brascan was the only palatable option to the former GNN executives. In their opinion, it was the only option that provided the formula for success, which was the mills being connected to the hydro system and the land (Griffin).

In 2012, Brookfield described itself on its website as a "global alternative asset manager with approximately $150 billion in assets under management." Brookfield is also the parent company of Great Lakes Hydro LLC, the company that owns GNP's old hydro system. Brookfield renamed the mills Katahdin Paper. Its initial plans for the Millinocket mill included a sixty-million-dollar thermomechanical pulping (TMP) operation. The TMP plant renders pulp into fiber and allows the glossy supercalendered paper that the Number Eleven paper machine produces to be made more efficiently (Turcotte). One company insider confided that at one point, TMP was purchased from a company in Quebec, shipped to Eastport, and then transported by rail to Millinocket (As a side note, Katahdin Paper eventually used groundwood from East Millinocket as part of Millinocket's turnaround. Groundwood is less expensive than TMP, but TMP produces a stronger fiber). Brookfield/ Katahdin Paper also suggested that two of Millinocket's other machines should be restarted. Number Eleven was restarted, but the other plans never materialized. The other machines that were potential restart candidates were torn out of the plant. An operator of a metal-recycling company, which did some of the removal work, told me that the only machine left in the plant was Number Eleven.

Brookfield/Katahdin Paper operated both mills, and it announced in 2007 that it intended to sell the Katahdin mills to Fraser Paper of

Madawaska, Maine. At the time, Brookfield owned 50 percent of Fraser, whose officials had assisted Brookfield in its initial assessment of the Katahdin mills and in performing management services. After Fraser's stockholders failed to approve the purchase of Katahdin, Brookfield reiterated its commitment to the Katahdin mills (Sambides Jr., 2007). Less than a year later, it announced the closure of the mill in Millinocket. The reason the company gave at the time was high oil prices (East Millinocket has a bark boiler installed by GNN that produces enough steam to easily run one of its two machines).

Company officials were quoted as saying that in 2007, the Millinocket mill consumed 400,000 barrels of oil (Sambides, 2008). Ironically enough, the proposed oil savings that Big A dam had promised was 438,000 barrels per year. Despite the high cost of oil, a company insider confided in me that the Millinocket mill had turned the corner financially, was profitable, and had a full book of orders for the remainder of the year.

The insider stated the Millinocket mill's turnaround was the result of three key items. The first was by reducing energy consumption. Teams went around the mill and found ways to reduce steam, water, and electric consumption, thus reducing oil consumption. They then improved the reliability of the machine by replacing hundreds of bearings on the various paper rolls. Finally, they increased the quality of the paper. One consumer tested the super-calendared paper from several companies and the paper from Number Eleven paper machine in Millinocket beat out the best in the world. The higher quality enabled Katahdin Paper to sell the product at a more profitable price.

Regardless of the success of the turnaround, the Millinocket mill was shut down in 2008. Brookfield publicly sought a partner to build and run a biomass boiler that would generate electricity and steam for the mill. But by 2010, no biomass boiler partner had been found, and Brookfield announced that it was seeking a buyer for the mills. As a side note, from the mid 1960s to 1986, the number three boiler in Millinocket burned a combination of wet bark from the wood room and oil (the dryer the bark the less oil was burned).

Number three boiler produced three-hundred thousand pounds of steam per hour running one third on wet bark. Had dry bark been used, a much higher percentage of the steam would have been produced by the bark, because it takes one thousand BTUs to remove one pound of water from bark. A retired power systems superintendent told me that had the company continued to burn the bark-oil combination, it would have contributed a significant amount of steam (not all that would be needed) for Number Eleven paper machine at a significant savings over oil alone (Fish). Also worth noting, the potential to make steam from electricity exists. East Millinocket's old steam plant had a boiler that operated on electricity. One engineer said that the dollar cost equivalent to a barrel of oil was less than forty dollars, thereby highlighting the opportunity cost involved with Inexcon selling the hydro system to remodel Number Eleven.

In February of 2011, Meriturn Partners, a restructuring and turnaround investor, signed a tentative agreement to purchase the mills. The agreement gave Meriturn less than sixty days to secure the necessary agreements and concessions needed to successfully turn around the mills. The reported sale price for the mills was one dollar, and the concessions that the towns were asked to give amounted to over forty million dollars over ten years (Sambides Jr., March 2011). Town officials told me that Meriturn initially wanted the two towns to reduce each mill's tax bill from over two million to approximately fifty thousand dollars. The state and town concession targets were never reached, but that wasn't the only factor that derailed the sale.

The paper business, like many large-scale manufacturing businesses, is very capital-intensive. Unfortunately, some of the owners since GNN didn't have the necessary capital to invest. Others showed little interest in making paper and appeared to acquire the mills for other assets that were part of a bigger package (Griffin).

Interestingly enough, as Meriturn was trying to negotiate for concessions, Brookfield shut down the East Millinocket mill and then said that if the company didn't sell the properties, both mills were going to be razed. East Millinocket's remaining customers withdrew their orders. With no customers, Meriturn "did not see a path to turn around the business," and the company withdrew on April 8, 2011 (Meriturn Partners).

Ultimately, Paul LePage, Maine's conservative Republican governor with some distant roots in the paper industry, negotiated a deal to delay the demolition of the mills and then helped to facilitate a sale to Cate Street Capital. Cate Street is an investment company that focuses on sustainable and environmentally friendly technology solutions. Part of the company's plan for the mills is to make bio-coal, or *torrefied wood*. In layman's terms: wood chips are cooked to eliminate moisture; when burned, the torrefied wood emits the heat of coal but with far fewer emissions.

It is a new beginning, but employment levels dropped from over six hundred in 2008 to about two hundred in 2012. At this point, the key is to stabilize those few remaining jobs and to pray that Cate Street makes enough money to justify starting the two machines that remained idle. Construction on the wood-torrefaction plant started in the fall of 2012. It is expected to initially generate twenty-five new jobs.

The Unions' Role

The skilled and loyal workforce that Great Northern had enjoyed for decades was a strong competitive advantage. GNP had a very unique apprentice program that developed its own human resource talent (Griffin). As time passed, a growing unrest and the tension between the younger trade union members and the papermakers' unions caused an unstable and expensive competitive disadvantage. Bill Laidig, GNN chairman, when talking about justifying capital investments, was quoted as saying, "To generate adequate returns requires the assurance of containing competitive manufacturing costs, and that means high productivity and rock-bottom manning in future GNP organizational arrangement. At every level, GNP management must establish and implement a philosophy that maximizes the utilization, productivity and skills of the work force" (Bartlett). Between the increased labor costs and the growing expense of the state's regulations, the southern United States became a more lucrative place to invest the profits from the Maine division of GNN.

Jim Giffune told me that despite the company's overwhelming generosity, it didn't handle its relations with labor well. Several management and union people told me that during GNN's "heyday," every couple of years, when talks would begin on new contracts, management would give the workers a raise. When the contract was signed, negotiators would get a steak dinner at the Great Northern guesthouse. Tom Griffin felt that a system in which labor shares in profits when the company does well and shares sacrifices when it doesn't would have been better for everyone (Griffin). Giffune said that, in hindsight, GNN should have sought more employee accountability via employee ownership. As an example, Cianbro, an employee-owned construction company, has over four thousand employees and has outperformed many of its original union-based competitors (Giffune). Prior to Inexcon's purchasing the mills, an employee buyout committee was formed. Some of the union members were skeptical about the process, and talks with the company sadly ended.

Owners of small businesses know that when a job needs doing, regardless of what it is or how long it will take, they do it. Those who don't have that attitude don't stay in business. When employees own the company they work for, there is no need for a union or union-work rules. This results in increased quality, efficiency, and lower labor costs.

The company's investments in its southern mills helped to maximize its profits. The South is perceived to have a more inviting business environment because many states have right-to-work laws and lower taxes. A former GNN manager, Warren Richardson, had the benefit of being a manager in a highly-unionized plant and also running the non-unionized Leaf River plant. He said that a non-unionized plant is not a manager's utopia, because the lack of a union structure presents a different form of labor problems. Negotiating wages, work rules, and discipline procedures with a union creates a structure from which to manage labor. Without a union, a manager has to be doubly sure of being perceived as fair and just (Richardson).

With that said, lower labor costs are seen as very desirable to a large company. The ability to better control labor costs in a weak or non-union climate derives from non-skilled labor's being much cheaper. Richardson said that skilled labor in Leaf River earned wages comparable to those of their counterparts in Maine.

While work rules can be helpful in some instances, in many instances union work rules can become archaic and inflexible (this does not mean that GNP's management was without fault). In the case of GNP, it resulted in higher labor costs per ton of paper. GNP's labor costs per ton of paper was 5.8 man hours in 1985, compared to 5 for Quebec, 4 for the U.S. South, and 3.7 for Finland. Some of the higher costs were the result of too many turn-of-the-century paper machines, but labor rules needed to be addressed in order for the company to survive (Bartlett). To their credit, local unions eventually modified work rules to help the company.

Labor relations have always been a strategic element of any successful business plan. In the case of GNP, salaries and wages comprised 40 percent of all of its costs (Bartlett). It is important to remember that unions gave us the forty-hour work week, safe working conditions, and fair pay. The sad thing is, when they won all these notable accomplishments, the national union bosses realized that unless they created something else to prove to the workers they still needed the union, the union bosses were going to be out of a job. So they convinced the workers they were getting shafted by "The Man." Across many industries, the unions pushed and pushed, and sometimes went on strike for the sake of having a strike. They did this until the workers had contracts that companies could no longer afford.

Great Northern Paper Company was not exempt from the wrath of these powerful unions. I have already mentioned GNP's unfailing generosity, but words cannot describe that generosity's far-reaching impact. Despite the terrific wages and benefits, and the fact that Great Northern built the Magic City, in the summer of 1978, some of the unions voted to go on strike. The strike lasted some two months, and the mill was forced to shut down.

John Dicenties, a member of the trades union representing mechanics, pipers, machinists, and carpenters, among others, and the co-chair of the union's negotiating team, said the trades unions and the papermakers unions voted to strike. Dicenties also said the four papermaker unions voted to go back to work sooner than the eight trades unions because the papermakers unions' strike fund didn't have enough money for an extended strike. The trades union members, however, had the ability to seek employment elsewhere in the construction field. That ability enabled the trades unions to remain on strike longer. The local credit union further enabled the strike by loaning money to strikers to help them with expenses while they were out of work.

The unions were offered a 22.2 percent pay increase over the next two years, but the papermakers unions were paid on a higher pay scale, and the trades unions wanted parity (McCann). Dicenties said that the papermakers union had a contract in place before the trades union finished negotiations. When the trades union got a bigger increase, the papermakers union demanded more money, and it kept going back and forth until the strike occurred. When John LaPoint, the federal mediator assigned to the case, was asked what made the negotiations so difficult, he reportedly said, "The cleavages between the locals and the hesitancy of the company to bridge the gap" (Slocum). The irony of the 1978 strike was that papermakers comprised two-thirds of the workforce, but because the voting system required each union one vote, a minority of the workers kept the mills shuttered.

It is very important to note that, regardless of how stressful the 1978 strike was, there was no violence on either side. Both sides respected for each other. Dicenties said that the Millinocket and East Millinocket mills had the best management crew that you could ask for. He said if a worker had a problem, he could go to the plant engineer or mill manager or even the president of the Maine mills to get it resolved. He said they were great to work for, because it was a team effort. Dicenties went on to say that he felt there was some sort of a gap or rift between the local management and corporate management that caused some of the problems that led to the 1978 strike.

After almost eight weeks, the strike began to affect the economy in northern Maine and was causing paper shortages throughout New England. Efforts by the governor and federal and state mediators failed to resolve the gridlock (Slocum). The strike ripped the town in two. Families were torn. (But some of the workers said it was the best summer they ever had, because the strike was like a two-month vacation.) The strike ended when Great Northern offered the trades unions an additional five cents per hour.

I have had retired union members tell me that they paid union dues for decades and the union never did anything for them. They felt that the union actually sold them down the river on various issues. In defense of any union that goes on strike, the union leadership seems to be good at creating dissatisfaction among the ranks. The leadership uses powerful arguments to "prove" that the workers are getting unfair treatment. Just one or two disgruntled employees act as yeast to bread; they affect the entire batch.

These arguments on the part of labor advocates and union leaders are as old as recorded history, and humans' dissatisfaction with their lot in life is just as old. Look at the book of Genesis in the Bible to see the first recorded example of these arguments and the first strike. In essence, Satan convinced Adam and Eve that God was holding out on them, and why shouldn't they share in what God had? Adam and Eve could hardly have had it better—they were in paradise, the Garden of Eden—but it didn't make any difference to them. And it didn't make any difference in the Magic City.

The direct cost of the strike to the company was an estimated ten million dollars (McCann). GNP's parent company, Great Northern Nekoosa, reported that the 1978 strike reduced paper shipments by 140,000 tons and cost the company sixty-five cents per share on its annual report (*Bangor Daily News*). A two-month curtailment in production in itself wasn't going to ruin Great Northern, but the side effects had a lasting impact. Just like the cost of winning an argument for a businessperson is a lost customer, the cost of "winning a strike" to a union member, in the long term, is often a lost job.

The 1978 strike prompted Great Northern's customers to scramble to find alternative sources of paper. This allowed other companies that would never have had the chance to get their foot in the door to take away GNN orders. According to an article written by former GNN human resource manager David Woodbury, not all of the orders came back, and some that did only returned partially. The customers, fearing future labor unrest, wanted to have a stable supply of paper, so they in essence divided their orders among two companies. A senior marketing analyst, David Roop, informed me that it seemed that even after the strike ended and production resumed, volumes never appeared to reach pre-strike levels. He said that when the strike started, GNN was number one in the directory paper market, and he knew of some directory orders that never returned. Those who went on strike and believed in the "principle" of the nickel raise that got them back to work only felt that Great Northern suffered a minor, short-term ding. The fact of the matter is that the company permanently lost some orders as a result of the 1978 strike, and thus the strike had long-term negative consequences.

Retired management personnel told me that the strike made it that much harder to justify capital investments in the Millinocket and East Millinocket mills. Dicenties said that if the company had a problem with the cost of labor, it was its own fault, because the company agreed to what the unions asked for. A company manager confided in me that corporate headquarters told local management, "Whatever you do, don't shut those machines down." A longtime Millinocket businessman said, "The company [GNP] had to have been giving away the store. I'd often hire someone, train them for six months, and then they would get an unskilled job in the mill paying twice what I could pay for doing skilled labor."

In the end, regardless of who was at fault, strikes are like nuclear war—no one wins. Strikes often have the same effect on businesses as a dog biting his master. The master will never fully trust that dog again. So how would the owners of Great Northern feel when the workers voted to strike? Especially after all the company had done for the workers and the town? Strikes make it much harder to sell the idea of capital investments to the board of directors. A lack of necessary investments leads to a lack of innovation and competitiveness, and a long-term lack of investment was one of the reasons a Great Northern successor was forced to shutter the plant in the Magic City.

The State's Role

In 1990, Georgia-Pacific paid for several key legislators to tour some of its southern mills. Included in the group were Maine state Senate president Charles Pray and state representative Mike Michaud, both Democrats from the Katahdin region. GP explained to the group that there were four key areas that prevented it from investing in Maine. The four intolerable conditions were:

1. Property taxes were too high,
2. Maine's workers' compensation rates were the highest in the nation,
3. The environmental permitting process was too long,
4. The cost of pulp in Millinocket was ten dollars a cord higher than in other states (Gerow).

Maine's poor business climate didn't happen overnight; it was the culmination of decades of heavy-handed politics. Liberal academic politicians replaced the pragmatic thinkers in Maine, and the results proved toxic to the economy (Griffin).

Property Taxes

Maine's tax burden was, and continues to be, one of the highest in the nation. In 2011, the combined tax burden of the mills in Millinocket and East Millinocket was $4.7 million (Sambides Jr., March 2011). Compare this figure with an average property tax bill for the Leaf River Mississippi mill—$300,000 to $400,000 in the 1990s (Richardson). Taxes were a significant factor in determining return on investment and the allocation of capital resources, but they were not the only factor. (As a side note, an internal GNP document showed that in 1975, Arkansas charged 1.3 cents of state taxes per dollar of paper sales, compared to Maine's much higher 4.4 cents of taxes per dollar of paper sales.)

Workers' Compensation

Another continuing attack on all businesses, but especially companies like GNP, was Maine's workers' compensation system. As the 1980s approached, the state of Maine placed additional burdens on its business community with revisions to its workers' compensation system. David Woodbury described those laws by arguing that "Maine made its own single greatest contribution to the decline of GNP" (Woodbury). Under

Governor Joseph Brennan in the 1980s, Maine's workers' compensation laws were significantly liberalized. One of the law firms that was influential in the development of the new laws ended up having one of its partners appointed to the position of Maine's attorney general. The firm opened an office in the Magic City in an effort to represent workers' claims against Great Northern. Great Northern had a self-insured workers' compensation fund that was paying out or reserving eleven million dollars per year for claims by the mid-1980s (Woodbury).

One GNP mill manager was summoned to GNN headquarters in Stamford, Connecticut, to explain "the ten-million-dollar charge" that was on the Millinocket mills' balance sheet every year; the charge was projected as far as the company could project (Giffune). Well, in the mid-1970s, the two Maine mills were responsible for almost 60 percent of the entire corporation's workers' compensation expense. Costs in the 1980s were even worse. GNP budgeted ten million dollars annually to cover this expense (Giffune.)

Several former managers told me that the problem became so blatant that the company could count on an increase in workers' compensation claims in October and November each year. Some workers would "injure" themselves each year near hunting season and be healed near the end of hunting season. The topic would often be an issue during managers' meetings. Some workers so frequently injured themselves that management expected it of them. The abuses were from a minority of employees, but the expenses were enormous, both in terms of treatment and lost productivity. The ten- to eleven-million-dollar charge was one of the reasons quality investors shunned GNN's Maine mills. When the costs were projected out, they totaled over one hundred million (Giffune). In 1980s dollars, that could cover the cost of rebuilding a paper machine.

Workers' compensation costs at GNN's mills in other states were measurably less. In 1982, workers' compensation rates in Maine cost employers $124 million—40 percent higher than the national average (Irwin Jr.,). By 1990, Maine was reported to have the highest workers' compensation premiums in the country (Gerow). Paul H. Kallop, a vice president and actuary (a risk and loss analyst), was quoted as saying, "Approximatly 30 percent of the state's premium is in the plan and approximatly 50 percent in the state's policies" (Irwin Jr.). When developing rates, insurance companies use multiple statistics, which include, but are not limited to, state policies on the benefit levels, what the state uses to determine full and partial disability, and actual lost work time.

The state's Bureau of Labor Standards reported that Maine ranked first in the nation for lost work time in 1982. Lost time is a double negative, because it raises compensation rates and lowers worker productivity.

In the preamble to the One Hundred Eleventh Legislature's LD 1322, "An Act to Reform Workers' Compensation System," the state of Maine admitted that its workers' compensation system was fraught with problems. The preamble states in part, "the Workers' Compensation System in Maine suffers from structural problems which cause higher costs to Maine employers and delays in benefits due Maine's injured workers." Unfortunately, the state wasn't able to lower employers' costs. Workers' compensation expenses were to remain out of control into the 1990s.

The state had debated the escalating workers' compensation expenses for several years. Changes and modifications didn't solve the crisis. During a 1982 workers' compensation debate, the Business Legislation Committee compared the state's approval-based system with a "competitive" rating system. In Maine's system, an insurance company had to seek approval for rate increases from the insurance superintendent. In a competitive rating system, the markets determine the price based on the level of competition. A good example of such a system would be the automobile insurance market. At the time, only two states, Minnesota and Oregon, had a competitive rating system for workers' compensation (Business Legislation Committee).

The 1983 *"Report of the Speaker's Select Committee on Worker's Compensation"* (SSC) quoted John Martin, Maine's Speaker of the House, as saying, "The cost of workers' compensation insurance coverage to Maine Employers is outrageous." He described the workers' compensation issue as "one of the issues most critical to establishing a more competitive business climate and improved employment opportunities in Maine...It fosters expensive litigation: long drawn-out court battles that neither side ever really wins...In short, the problem with the system, as I see it, is the system itself."

The reason the SSC was formed was that the relative rates of workers' compensation in Maine were high. From 1970 to 1981, approved rates had increased 336 percent, and from 1978 to 1981, rates increased an average of 21.9 percent annually (Speaker's Select Committee on Workers' Compensation). The number one recommendation of the SSC was that the state should implement an early pay system. The premise of an early pay system is that paying an employee early and providing prompt medical treatment and therapy eliminates an adversarial relationship between the claimant and the payer (Speaker's Select Committee on Workers' Compensation).

In an effort to control costs, Great Northern developed safety teams and incentives for reaching safety goals, but costs continued to be oppressive. One of the main culprits was a 1983 workers' compensation reform law that took effect in 1984. A former human resource director, David Woodbury, summed up the changes by stating, "The firm of McTeague, Higbee, Libner, et al., in Topsham succeeded in getting substantial changes in Maine's workers' compensation law through the legislature and signed by Governor Brennan. Then the firm was fortunate to see one of its own partners, Jim Tierney, appointed Attorney General for Maine" (Woodbury). The McTeague law firm came to Millinocket and encouraged its clients to seek full compensation under the workers' compensation law.

Patrick McTeague was legal counsel to the Maine AFL-CIO. In 1984, he spoke at the Maine Summer Labor Institute. McTeague was quoted as saying, "We in Maine have begun to change the system." He went on to say that higher workers' compensation rates are a good thing, because the best way to cut down on work-related injuries "is to make them expensive." He also targeted paper companies, shipbuilders, and large contractors as having "the balance of power." One interesting thing that he cited was that when a company insures workers by using a private insurance company, the "overhead costs are often twice as expensive as when a company self-insures itself [sic]" (Lobozzo). It is important to note that GNP's workers' compensation fund was a self-insured account like those McTeague spoke of. Using his statistics, we can conclude that, had GNP hired a private insurance company, it would have cost fifteen million dollars.

The revised law did little to control costs, but it provided injured workers with improved benefits and legal representation; workers were soon seeking six-figure settlements. Woodbury cited a case in which a worker in his twenties sustained a back injury while at work. He went directly to the hospital, where cocaine was discovered in his blood. The workers' compensation board discounted the presence of cocaine, and the worker was given a total disability settlement. The company was also prevented from taking disciplinary action against the worker "because the employee was not tested for cause." The employee took the money from the settlement and started a business on the coast (Woodbury).

The legislation was intended to lower and control costs, but in reality it did neither. The new law provided injured employees with two-thirds of their pay without taxes while they were out of work. The system was improved to facilitate prompt payments to injured workers. Workers' compensation payments are not taxed, because they are insurance payouts, not wages, and therefore the employee's net compensation is almost as much as his or her normal net wage after taxes. In some instances, employees were determined to have a level of disability severe enough that they were thus entitled to a settlement. Former management personnel and other small-business owners told me that some employees found it more enjoyable to receive two-thirds pay or a large settlement for no work rather than working.

The legislation further encouraged employees to return to work on "light duty." While on light duty at work, some were still well enough to engage in heavy-duty activities at home. Other employees became envious of injured coworkers' reduced workloads, manifesting in lower productivity. In a small town, people see the abuses, and the natural question that some asked was, "Why should I work harder so that someone else doesn't have to?" Some people who got large settlements seemed to be miraculously healed by them. Only a minority of the employees abused the system, but the compensation they received comprised an enormous amount of the total cost.

Former GNN personnel told me that when GNN compared its several operating divisions with its GNP subsidiary, workers' compensation costs were one of the factors affecting the allocation of capital investment funds. The Maine mills lost out on needed capital investments, partly because its workers' compensation costs were 40 percent higher than the national average. The lack of investment is a recurring theme in the economic destruction of Millinocket.

Unintended Consequences of Uncertainty

Starting in the late 1960s to the early 1970s, there was a marked change in the attitude toward business in the state. The state went from encouraging the betterment of its residents through investment in business to antagonizing businesses with ever-changing standards. Tom Sawyer, a retired president of Sawyer Environmental, said that when he was in business in Maine, about every five years or so he had to undertake a significant strategic change in his business. I said to him, "I bet it is because of the government." He replied, "Always because of the government."

Great Northern was sensing a shift in public attitudes due to pressure from environmental activists. Activists were criticizing paper companies' management and care of the forests, public lots, and the rivers. Although GNP was the single largest economic engine in northern Maine and a good steward of the land, it was forced into numerous costly battles that diverted attention from its operations. When the company wasn't spending millions of dollars defending itself from attacks, it was spending millions redeveloping its operations to meet new regulations.

In the late 1960s and early 1970s, environmentalists started a campaign to force the end of log drives. For centuries, rivers were used to transport logs from the forest to the mills for processing, and Maine was no exception. Environmentalists claimed that the bark from the logs was clogging the rivers and therefore harming the fish. Great Northern saw the inevitable end to the log drives, partially because the availability of labor to conduct river drives and to cut wood into four-foot lengths was shrinking. Another major factor was regulatory change forced a costly alternative to traditional log drives. Converting to tree-length logs and trucking them was the only feasible alternative. The result was the Golden Road, a network of 3,500 miles of roads that traversed GNP's 2.1 million acres of forest.

Building and maintaining the Golden Road was an enormous capital expense. With setbacks and ditches, much of the road is approximately fifty feet wide. The construction of the road, therefore, removed approximately twenty thousand acres of productive forest. Beforehand, the only way to reach some of these areas was to hike or fly in. Now, two million acres of land are open to the family sedan, introducing extra fishing and hunting pressures in previously remote areas.

Maintaining the road for logging trucks and sports created another financial burden. Few companies had to build such an enormous road network, let alone maintain one (Giffune). In Mississippi, the state and county paid to maintain logging roads (Richardson). It was just another reason the South was more attractive.

Initially, the log drives were not only authorized by the state of Maine but were actually encouraged. That long history got lost to the political winds (Giffune). The environmentalists got their way, but fishing didn't improve. I've interviewed numerous lifelong fishermen and hunters from Millinocket's Fin & Feather Club, and they insist that the fishing on the West Branch was better when there were active log drives in the Penobscot. I've also interviewed fishermen from the Miramichi River in New Brunswick, Canada, and they say the same thing. The fishermen's theory is that the logs have bugs on them, which provide food for the fish, and when the logs are going down the rivers they dredge out small areas that serve as pools or resting areas for the fish. Also worth noting is that, though the Miramichi is unobstructed by dams, the salmon runs have gone from being so thick in the early 1900s that you could shoot them with a rifle to being so rare that one can fish for days without catching a salmon.

One of the key proponents of the ban on log drives was a Republican by the name of Howard Trotzky. He was motivated to end them in the early 1970s when he discovered a large number of logs and bark in the Penobscot River. He filed a lawsuit to end the practice. The state and federal governments eventually joined in, and log drives were officially banned in 1976. Trotzky was also influential in another of Maine's key environmental and regulatory landmarks. Joe Brennan, Maine's Democratic governor from 1979 to1987, nominated Richard Barringer as conservation commissioner, and Trotzky was the deciding vote to confirm him (Smith).

In 1972, a young Barringer wrote an influential book entitled *A Maine Manifest*. Barringer is an intelligent man who has had an impressive career in government and education. Some of his accomplishments, as listed by the University of Southern Maine's Muskie School of Public Service, include teaching a course called "Foundations of Public Policy, Sustainable Communities, and Environmental Policy." He has served as director of state planning and as commissioner of conservation.

A Maine Manifest listed Maine's superior shipping ports as prospects for creating economic growth. He suggested carefully selecting one or two for shipping purposes. In his campaign for governor in 2010, Bill Beardsley stressed the importance of Maine's ports, the closest ports to Europe on the East Coast. Therefore, one might conclude that Barringer's plan in the 1970s was ahead of its time.

The troubling part of *A Maine Manifest* involved policy suggestions and strategies for preferred growth. He suggested that preservation of land was a better use of it than most forms of development. He also suggested that Maine should remain as it was, preserved for future generations. In order to achieve that goal, the book seemed to encourage institutions whose main purpose was to curb some forms of development (Barringer).

The biggest threat to the paper companies was his proposed land banks. Part of his vision was for the state to acquire land and then lease it out in such a fashion as to generate income and to control development that would be deemed undesirable. On page 70, he specifically wrote about how paper companies would find it profitable to make land donations to the state and take the tax loss. Visions such as these led to policies that placed new pressures on companies like GNN, and as a result, new capital investments became even more sporadic.

As the 1970s unfolded, paper companies, including Great Northern, became the center of a nasty political battle that involved the management of public lots. When Maine sold land to the paper and timber companies in the 1800s, it maintained rights to a lot within each township. These lots are referred to as public lots. When the state needed money to fund projects, it would often sell cutting rights to the lands (McCann).

At some point in the 1970s, harvesting practices on the public lots were challenged. In the early 1980s, the Maine Supreme Court ruled that the timber-cutting rights that were granted in the 1800s had expired and that the state now owned those rights (Cleaves). The court's decision opened the door for fines for the paper companies and negotiations with the state to minimize them. The state negotiated a value-for-value land swap for the lots, thus giving the state credit as if it owned the public lots outright. The state chose lots in what it deemed more desirable locations. Former GNP executive Jim Giffune said, "The most ironic part of this travesty is that there was more wood on GNP's public lots at the time of the court case than there was when they were granted." Given that, Giffune asked the question, "What do you suppose GNN's officers and directors thought about the state's decision?"

While there was a change in the cadence of capital investments, and despite profits from the Maine mills being used to improve other divisions of the company, GNN did try to make other significant investments in the Maine operation. In the mid-1970s, there were plans to build a kraft mill between the two Maine mills (*kraft* is one of the main ingredients in paper). At the time, most of Great Northern's paper was composed of about 70 percent ground wood (which is just a log ground up into short fibers that comprise the bulk of a sheet of paper but are too weak to make a strong sheet), 20 to 22 percent sulfite-derived fiber, and the remainder was kraft. Kraft fiber is usually bleached, and is therefore brighter than the sulfite fiber that GNN used. It is more expensive to produce than sulfite, but a bleached kraft fiber is necessary for high-quality coated papers. It is important to note that people familiar with the industry tell me that the last kraft mill built in Maine was constructed in the mid-1970s.

Kraft has the ability to utilize hardwood and therefore offers the benefit of full-fiber utilization. The kraft mill was to be built near Dolby Pond, and it would have created a better use of the company's fiber and would have made the Maine division a more viable asset for the future. The company made two requests of the state. One was that it wanted to be exempt from paying sales tax on the materials used in the construction of the plant, and the other involved the water that was to be used in the manufacture of kraft. Because of the location of the proposed plant, the company wanted to use water from the East Branch of the Penobscot, process the kraft pulp, and then treat the water and discharge it into the West Branch.

The water discharged into the West Branch meets the East Branch about one to two miles downstream. The kraft plant would have provided jobs and a significant long-term tax base to the local and state economy. Despite the advantages, the state's environmental regulations disallowed taking water from one body and discharging it into another. State regulations only allow discharging water back into the same body of water that it came from. Even though the East Branch and the West Branch meet up about a mile downstream, they were considered two different bodies of water.

The state also refused to provide a sales tax exemption. The combination of higher taxes, higher labor costs, and more costly regulations made the program too costly. GNN killed the Maine kraft mill and instead chose a more lucrative proposal in 1977. In the end, GNN built the kraft mill in Arkansas because locating it there offered a much better return on investment. Former managers said that the company never seriously considered the Dolby kraft mill project, because most of the grades of paper that the company was producing at the time didn't require the more expensive kraft and the northern project had a perceived poor return on investment in comparison with the southern alternative.

The state was dumbfounded. James Longley, Maine's governor from 1975 to 1979, demanded that the president of the Great Northern division of GNN explain Northern's decision. Retired chief engineer Wes Nash, who was privy to the presentation, explained it to me. At the time, the three divisions of GNN were all performing about on par with each other. (As a side note, keep in mind that it was the profits from the Maine mills that refurbished the old Nekoosa mills and built the new mills of the Great Southern division.) The Northern division was paying almost half of the entire corporation's tax liability. More importantly, the Northern division was responsible for over half of the workers' compensation expenses.

I have seen internal GNP notes, which listed several factors that made the Ashdown, Arkansas, plant more lucrative: The capital costs for a turnkey plant in Ashdown was significantly less due to non-union construction labor. The energy costs in Ashdown were half as much, because the plant used coal instead of oil. Finally, Arkansas had a significant advantage in the cost of wood (this will be discussed in another section).

Throughout the 1970s, Great Northern viewed the government's treatment of the company as a series of attacks. One of the attacks was from Mother Nature, and it came in the form of a spruce budworm epidemic. When a spruce forest ages, it becomes more susceptible to this infestation, which ruined thousands of acres, and had the company not sprayed pesticides, it most likely would have been worse. Spraying two million acres cost millions each year.

When the budworms ravaged an area, vast swaths of trees would die. The only thing to do was to spray the forest and to try and cut the trees down before they were destroyed. The outbreak of the tiny worms wasn't the state's fault, but former officials said that while the company was trying to save its forest, it was criticized by environmentalists, who didn't like some of the chemicals used to fight the pests and the ensuing wholesale cutting of trees. The resulting political pressures led the state to increase environmental regulations, which resulted in increased costs for the company.

Indian Land Claims

Another irritant to GNP, the Indian Land Claims, came about in the late 1970s. A young lawyer by the name of Tom Tureen, representing Native American interests, was trying to return two-thirds of the entire state of Maine (twelve million acres, valued at twenty-five billion dollars) to the Native Americans (Blagden). The Penobscot and Passamaquoddy tribes asserted that because the eastern states dealt with the tribes on a state-by-state basis, the states were in violation of the federal Nonintercourse Act of 1790. The basis of the claim was that large amounts of Indian land were transferred to the state of Maine without the consent of the US Congress. There was a real possibility that the Indians were going to win their claim.

President Jimmy Carter eventually intervened and negotiated a settlement with the tribes, but not before the case became a potential nightmare for every landowner in northern Maine. In the end, the Indian Land Claims Act cost the government eighty-one million dollars when the final settlement was made in 1980 (Turkel). As part of the settlement, GNP and other landowners agreed to sell parcels of timberland to the tribes. GNN owned over two million acres of forest; the uncertainty over those three years was a serious threat to its business model. Fighting the absurd lawsuit took up a substantial amount of manpower and resources that could have been better used elsewhere in the company.

The settlement was supposed to improve the welfare of the Native Americans and help lift them out of poverty. Former GNN officials and other Maine businesspeople that I interviewed said that the case was nothing more than a money grab. Thirty years later, many of the members of the tribes still live in poverty.

Big A

In 1986, Energy costs for GNP's "marginal tonnage" (production that was run on a month-to-month basis and periodically shut down due to demands in the marketplace and high costs) carried costs that were seventy dollars per-ton higher than its normal production. GNN's chairman Bill Laidig, in talking about capital investment was quoted as saying, "The hard fact is that GNP cannot obtain corporate commitment for additional investment unless the financial returns are competitive" (Bartlett). Higher-than-average operational costs are a deterrent to investment, but the state's environmental regulations were also an obstacle to capital investments. Maine's environmental regulations played an instrumental part in preventing GNP from building a much-needed kraft pulp mill in the mid-1970s. Then, in the early to mid-1980s, Great Northern proposed a hydroelectric dam on the Penobscot River just a few miles south of Ripogenus Dam. The initial studies were conducted in the 1970s, but because the most feasible location flooded out a small section of Baxter State Park, GNP concluded that the state wouldn't allow construction, and the plan was tabled. The dam that was eventually proposed didn't actually provide the best return on investment, but it was viewed as the most saleable.

The project, a thirty-six-megawatt hydroelectric dam, was referred to as "Big A" after the river's Big Ambejackmockamus Falls. The dam would have indeed flooded the rapids in the gorge, but it would have produced a deep eight-hundred-acre cold-water lake. The company projected that it would have cost almost one hundred million dollars to construct. GNP also spent a great deal of time and money studying the potential effects of the project on the salmon fishery and other recreational industries. Its studies showed how the white-water rafting companies could develop a profitable business model by offering rafting trips south of the proposed dam.

The dam was partially the result of an internal conflict at the company. Great Northern's management saw the benefits and absolute necessity of a new paper machine, to produce higher-quality paper at a lower cost. The original idea was to shut down some of the old labor-intensive machines in favor of a new one. But the sales staff wanted to keep the old machines running, because the business-forms grades of paper that those machines produced at the time were lucrative. The problem was that the addition of the Number Eleven paper machine in 1972 maxed out the production capacity of the groundwood and pulping facilities of the Millinocket mill. The only way to increase capacity was to add new groundwood and pulping facilities (Johnson).

Additional groundwood capacity required an enormous amount of power. That power could have been derived from condensing power from GNP's high-pressure steam system. This would have required additional steam capacity, which would have required burning an enormous amount of oil in a power-generation facility. The alternative was hydropower. Because it is relatively inexpensive, it was the only feasible way to generate the necessary power (Johnson). Big A was therefore seen as the first step in transforming the Maine mills into highly competitive operations.

It is important to remember that Great Northern and the United States had just endured two major oil shocks in the 1970s, and the power that this proposed dam could have produced would have had a major impact on reducing operating costs, besides providing the company with constant and reliable power. GNP was also planning several upgrades that would have been financially justified because of the power generated from the dam. Existing hydroelectric power is the cleanest, most reliable, and cheapest form of power, far cheaper than wind power. Once established, hydro produces electricity at just under one cent per kilowatt (Texas Comptroller of Public Accounts).

A 2012 report by the American Tradition Institute estimated the true cost of onshore wind to be between fifteen and nineteen cents per kilowatt-hour. Normal figures for wind don't include the cost of backup resources that are required to produce electricity when the wind isn't blowing (Brown). Big A would have enabled Great Northern to produce large amounts of clean, renewable power. It would have justified using an energy-dependent process that would have allowed the company to make a much more efficient use of its trees. One would think that the environmentalists would have cheered such a move, but they couldn't get in line fast enough to oppose it.

The Big A proposal became a national fight. Newspapers from far away, such as the *Los Angeles Times*, reported on the proposal. Chris Brown, acting head of the Washington-based American Rivers Conservation Council, was quoted in the *Los Angeles Times* as saying, "Our feeling is the Penobscot is the most threatened river in the country…It's a national treasure. It's probably the only river that I've been rafting on where you can dip your cup into the water and drink." Brown was the spokesman for eight national conservation groups that fought the Big A proposal (Drogin). Interestingly enough, rafting on that section of the Penobscot River is made possible by Ripogenus Dam, constructed by GNP in 1915 and providing consistent water flows throughout the dry summer months. Experts familiar with the West Branch of the Penobscot tell me that the natural water flow in the dry-summer months would not sustain white-water rafting. The dam was originally constructed to facilitate the log drives, but in the early 1950s, a hydroelectric generating facility was connected to the dam.

The company chartered buses to take people to Augusta, Maine's capital, to testify in favor of the project. It also had all the scientific research to show the possible effects of the dam and how the project would benefit its operation and the community. Former Maine Governor John Baldacci, Democrat of Bangor, earlier made a name for himself leading the opposition to Big A. To this day, several environmental groups cite as their claim to fame the success they had in stopping the Big A project. They used emotional objections to fight the scientific research. I remember one of my middle school teachers saying, "They didn't need the dam anyway, because they couldn't use all the power it produced and it would have destroyed the river." She didn't know the company's proprietary plans, nor did she take into account the numerous other dams on the river that were in place before she was born. These dams still allowed some of the best freshwater stream fishing for coldwater game fish in the eastern United States.

There is a difference of opinion on whether Big A was essential to the long-term needs of the company. Some claim that the increased profits that the dam would have produced would have guaranteed necessary future investments. The increased investment would have guaranteed profitability for decades. Some senior managers unequivocally state that, had the company simply invested in a bleached-kraft mill and added one or two modern paper machines, the Maine division would have continued to be viable.

The addition of new machines would have required eliminating several old machines of an equal amount of production capacity. Two new machines could produce more paper than ten of Millinocket's old machines (Gerow). It would have meant keeping far fewer employees—but still considerably more than zero. The paper grades that the old machines excelled at steadily became unprofitable as increased computer usage significantly reduced the demand for paper. In this instance, Big A wouldn't have been pivotal, but former executives say that the dam still would have been desirable. It is worth noting that when GNP was relicensing its hydro dams in the late 1980s and early 1990s, the company spent years and millions of dollars to obtain the licenses. The company even had to fund numerous studies and even archeological projects to satisfy some of the interested parties (Carson). Given the removal of some hydroelectric dams in southern Maine since 2000, it appears that environmental advocates are willing to badger some dam owners into selling their dams and having them removed over renewing the licenses and continuing operation. When existing hydroelectric capacity is removed, it has to be replaced by a more expensive form of electricity, because making power with natural gas, wind, solar, oil, or biomass is more expensive than existing hydropower. It goes without saying that the increased electric costs are a deterrent to business development.

Charles Pray, the former president of the Maine state Senate and a Millinocket native, has long argued that GNN never intended to build the Big A dam. He claims that the Maine legislature passed legislation that would have allowed the construction of the dam that included some environmental trade-offs, such as fish ladders. Pray said that GNN simply wanted to protect its right to build the dam, thereby preventing other parties from constructing a dam on that stretch of the Penobscot River. Federal regulations at the time would have permitted anyone to file a permit for a dam on that stretch of the Penobscot. GNN's filing was designed to thwart a third party from placing a dam in the middle of GNN's enormous hydro system.

In his book *Timber!: The Fall of Maine's Paper Giant*, Paul McCann, former director of public relations at Great Northern Paper, lists the failure to build the Big A dam as one of the causes of GNN's demise. The dam was going to have a thirty-six-megawatt power station that would have reduced the company's oil consumption by 438,000 barrels per year. Had the dam been online in 1983, it would have lowered the company's energy cost of producing a ton of paper on five old machines to fifty-nine dollars. At the time, GNN's Canadian competition was paying sixty-eight dollars per ton to produce a similar grade (McCann). A former GNP president, Robert Bartlett, described the need for the dam in order for the Maine mills to remain competitive. He said that there was overcapacity of paper in the world, and that papermakers in Finland earned half as much as Maine workers. Workers in Brazil made even less, and that country's fast-growing eucalyptus trees mature in as few as fifteen years, compared with over thirty years for trees in Maine (Platt).

In 2010, Brookfield Asset Management, the owner of the Millinocket mills, reported that it lost approximately thirty million dollars in the almost eight years that it owned the properties. By contrast, Big A's reduced oil consumption (with crude prices at eighty dollars per barrel) would have translated to thirty-five million dollars in annual savings.

In the end, Maine's Land Use Regulation Commission (LURC) attached numerous conditions to the project. Two of the conditions contested by GNN were a "no job losses" order and a mandated energy audit (Associated Press, 1985). Despite the capital investments that the dam would have allowed, a "no job losses" condition would have been impossible to live up to. Any of the modernization plans would have improved efficiency, and so they would have led to a reduction in employment levels. But a modernization would have also allowed the mills to be more competitive in the future, in turn leading to a higher level of employment than there is now. No business can guarantee a specified number of jobs over a long period of time, because jobs are dictated by circumstances and the economy. At the time, the company had an almost ninety-year history of investing in Maine and providing employment, but that wasn't good enough for LURC. It wanted more.

The energy audit was intended to see if the company could more efficiently operate the plant. Members of LURC and critics of the plan felt that if enough energy savings could be realized, the dam might not have been needed. Company officials viewed it as a costly delay tactic. Governor Brennan was quoted as saying that the conditions violated the spirit of the "one-stop shopping" concept for hydro permits under the 1983 Maine Rivers Act (Associated Press, 1985).

The Declaration of Policy section of the 1983 Maine Rivers Act states, in item 6, Hydropower development: "Streamline procedures to facilitate hydropower development under reasoned environmental, technical, and public safety constraints" (Maine legislature). The Rivers Act goes on to state, in subarticle 1-B, permits for hydropower projects, that "hydropower development utilizing these waters is unique in its benefits and impacts to the natural environment, and makes a significant contribution to the general welfare of the residents of the state for the following reasons." Three detailed reasons are given as to why hydropower is beneficial to the people of the state:

1. Hydropower is the state's only economically feasible, large-scale energy resource that doesn't rely on combustion of a fossil fuel, and therefore avoids pollution problems.
2. Hydropower can have positive environmental impacts. For example, hydropower dams can control flood waters, improve water flows, increase water quality and recreational opportunities.
3. Hydropower is the state's only most significant indigenous resource that can be used to free Mainers from their extreme dependence on foreign oil.

The next section of the law describes that "hydropower justifies singular treatment" and that a simple and streamlined process should be in place for permits for the construction of hydro-generation facilities (Maine legislature). Brennan suggested that LURC should have voted the proposal up or down and that all of the conditions imposed by state agencies amounted to "too much intrusion" (Associated Press, 1985). The union members realized that modernizing the Millinocket mill would mean fewer jobs, but they were still traversing the state in an effort to build support for the project.

Former Great Northern president Robert F. Bartlett was quoted in the *Bangor Daily News* as saying, "I don't feel that what LURC did represents the feeling of the legislature or the whole state." He was further quoted as saying that GNN didn't get that type of hassle in Mississippi or in Wisconsin (Platt). Bartlett went on to complain about GNN having to undergo another process with the Department of Environmental Protection (DEP) to get a "water-quality certificate" before it could seek permission to construct the dam from the Federal Energy Regulatory Commission (FERC). It was Bartlett's view that the legislature intended that once a permit was issued, the DEP would issue the water-quality certificate (Platt). That is a reasonable conclusion, because the DEP was to be the primary issuer of permits unless a proposal was to be under the jurisdiction of LURC.

When the DEP denied GNN the necessary water-quality certificate several weeks after LURC issued the permit, Governor Brennan again claimed that the process violated the "one-stop shopping" provision of the 1983 Maine Rivers Act (Adams). The legislature tried to find a legislative solution to the problem, but in the end the proposal died. A couple of weeks before DEP rejected GNN's request for a permit, the head of the State Planning Office, Richard Barringer, released a progress report on the Maine Rivers Act and concluded that the "one-stop shopping" provision was working well (Associated Press, 1985).

This is the same Richard Barringer who, in *A Maine Manifest* a decade earlier, argued that most of Maine should be preserved for future generations "as is." He also proposed a land-bank concept, whereby large landowners like GNP would find it beneficial to give land to the state and take the tax loss. It was Barringer's view that a large landowner would incur less long-term expense by giving the land to the state rather than maintaining ownership of it. Barringer apparently felt that increased regulations would make the land less profitable, and that companies, therefore, would consider large tracts of land a liability rather than an asset.

Maine's State Planning Office, which Barringer was in charge of in the mid-1980s, is part of the Executive Department and was created in 1968. It was designed to provide the governor and legislature with independent analysis on the conservation of Maine's natural resources and the development of the state's economy. The State Planning Office's website describes its duties thusly: "The Maine State Planning Office strives to integrate the development of the State's economy with the conservation of its natural resources. This involves coordinating a long-range view of state policies; including the development of economic, natural resource, energy, land use, and fiscal and regulatory policy." In 2012, its mission was "to help build a sustainable future for Maine communities, businesses, and residents." Given the duties of the State Planning Office, the failure of GNP to feasibly construct Big A was a colossal failure for the people of Maine.

A former Millinocket town councilor says that environmental activists' approach is to "apply endless pressure endlessly." The eventual defeat of the Big A project was a major coup for environmental groups at the expense of the economy of northern Maine. By attaching numerous and unrealistic conditions to the permit, state officials were able to say to the business community that a permit was issued. They were also able to say to environmental activists that the numerous conditions and delays in the process amounted to a poison pill to the proposal. Paul McCann's account of the Big A saga credited Maine's House of Representatives with quickly passing a bill that would allow the project to continue without the LURC conditions, but the fight got bogged down in the Senate. Without a decisive mandate, the company withdrew from the fight on March 13, 1986 (McCann).

The failure of Great Northern to construct the Big A dam left the company in a precarious situation. Depending on whom you ask, Great Northern spent between six million and eight million dollars trying to get the dam approved. Several Great Northern managers and engineers claimed that had the "no jobs lost" clause been removed, the dam would have been constructed. It had funds allocated for the project, but it wasn't allowed to proceed. The company's fight garnered national attention, and the loss not only highlighted the high production costs of the Maine mills but also reaffirmed Maine's poor business climate to the entire business community. By the end of the 1980s, despite having a strong balance sheet, GNN's stock price was depressed and it became a prime target for a hostile takeover.

In the end, environmental forces, both internal and external to state government, killed a proposal that would have eliminated the need for four hundred thousand barrels of oil. The company spent millions of dollars trying to become more competitive by employing an environmentally friendly process, but the environmental forces had a bigger plan in view.

The Cost of Pulp

The enormous size of GNP's holdings in Maine made it a lightning rod for attacks from numerous special-interest organizations. Each of these attacks added incrementally to the cost of obtaining pulp wood. The attacks came in different forms. Several factors, including environmental pressures, caused the end of the river drives. The end of the river drives meant that GNP had to undertake a significant capital expenditure to make a couple of thousand miles of logging roads to service a million acres of forest that previously was serviced by river drives. The logging roads in the South were paid for by the state governments.

In the mid-1970s, the Maine Woodsman Association (MWA) was formed. It was comprised of woodcutters and contractors that were seeking to organize for the purpose of obtaining better pay rates from the paper and lumber companies. Wood workers were traditionally paid on piece rate. The pulp wood was cut into four-foot lengths peeled and stacked four feet high. It was the job of the scalers to measure the piles and make sure that the cutters' measurements were accurate.

MWA organized some small civil actions against the paper companies, but the lawsuits didn't achieve dramatic results. What MWA did do was attract the eye of Pine Tree Legal, which provides legal assistance to low income Mainers. Pine Tree Legal embraced MWA's cause and was successful in lobbying the state of Maine to get new scaling regulations implemented. The first set of scaling laws that the state of Maine implemented were not practical and were very difficult to implement. Two years later, the state revised the laws and GNN personnel were instrumental in developing workable rules.

Former GNN woodlands manager of information systems, Lewis House IV, helped to draft the new rules. He told me that parts of the requirements were that scalers had to be state-licensed and the state seals and measurements could check the scales to make sure they are accurate. Wood went from being cut in four-foot lengths to being cut in tree lengths. (It is worth noting that due to the end of the river drives, it was more efficient to cut and transport tree-length logs.) House and four crews of scalers measured trees and developed intricate scaling tables to accurately measure the volume of wood in a tree.

Trees have a tendency to flare near the base, and the scales were based upon cutting trees a specific height off the ground. Through statistical analysis, House and his team determined that a tree with a ten-inch butt had on average a specific volume of wood. In other words, they measured the diameter of the butt and not the length of the tree to determine the volume. In the summer, workers would get a slight premium because they cut the trees as close to the ground as possible, and in the winter, because of the snow, they had a slight reduction in pay because the trees were cut higher and away from the flare.

About the same time Pine Tree Legal was lobbying to implement scaling laws, the United Papermakers International Union (UPIU) organized the GNN woods camps. UPIU organized some sit-down strikes at the camps in protest of the scaling rules. They also complained to the state, claiming that the woodcutters were getting cheated because of the scaling tables.

The state investigated the scaling charges; and in an effort to prove their case, many of the woodcutters deliberately cut the trees higher than normal to exaggerate the reduced size. House escorted two state officials to the test area and showed them the exaggeratedly high stumps in the test area and the very low stumps when the cutters went back to work after the test was completed. The state could never prove that the GNN scaling tables were cheating the woodcutters, but a couple of years later, the state banned tree-length scaling. About the same time, GNN did away with its woods camps. All parties eventually agreed that while not perfect, weighing the wood was the best way to measure the volume.

When UPIU organized the woods camps, the cost of production generally went up. The state's increased regulation of how wood was measured also caused costs to go up. GNN's additional lobbying and administrative costs were also a burden. House told me that his budget was about half a million dollars and about one third of that overhead was dedicated to wood measurement and the check-scale group.

GNN contracted smaller companies to cut the wood after it stopped running its own camps. The smaller companies, Pelletier, Gardner, and Bouchard, were non-union and tended to have fewer camp foremen than GNN did. The unionization of the camps was a backdoor attack from the environmental groups to increase regulations. (It is important to remember that these events transpired during an outbreak of spruce budworm that destroyed thousands of acres of forest. The company employed clear cutting and spraying of pesticides to help mitigate the damage. Environmental groups tried various tactics to stop both practices.)

Internal GNP notes from a January 1978 meeting with Maine Governor James Longley outline the significant differences between the cost of pulp wood in Maine versus other states. In addition to higher labor costs, the cost of building woods roads, operating remote logging camps, plowing snow, and carrying winter inventory were not present in Arkansas. One chart showed a base cost of 100 percent for the cost per cord of pulp wood in Arkansas in 1972 and GNP's Maine cost was 125 percent. By 1978, those costs rose to 150 percent and 225 percent respectively.

Increased regulations, unionization, and workers' compensation costs made it more expensive to harvest trees, placing Maine's paper companies at a disadvantage against out-of-state competitors. When capital improvements were being planned, these price disadvantages were one of the factors that led GNN (and its successors) to favor other regions over its Maine mills.

Endless Pressure Endlessly Applied

Just two years after the environmental groups successfully defeated the Big A project, Patrick Leahy, D., Vermont, attached the Northern Forest Lands Study to a federal appropriations bill, without public hearings. The project, which was supported by the National Audubon Society, the Wilderness Society, the Sierra Club, and the Adirondack Council, among others, would create a park that covered twenty-six million acres, stretching from Downeast Maine to northern New York (Arnold).

By 1991, the study had been completed, and Senator Leahy's staff, with the help of Brock Evans of the National Audubon Society, drafted the Northern Forest Lands Act of 1991. The proposal included millions of dollars for creating a four-state forestlands inventory and nationalizing forestlands. That same year, Senators William Cohen and George Mitchell, the Senate majority leader, both of Maine, held informational hearings on the Northern Forest Lands Project in Maine (Arnold). Henry Joy, an eight-term representative to the Maine legislature, told me that once people became aware of the ramifications of the radical environmental proposal, they were furious and let their feelings be known to the Maine senators. Landowners and small-business owners quickly realized that such a federally-sponsored land grab would eliminate future development and suffocate an already struggling economy. Cohen and Mitchell both pulled any support that they may have had for the project and worked to kill the proposal.

Not wanting to wait for the federal government, or perhaps smelling defeat, the Natural Resources Council of Maine (NRCM) and the Maine Audubon Society proposed a 10.5-million-acre North Woods conservation area. NRCM went to the extremes of asking LURC to "downzone the state's unorganized townships, forest plantations, and coastal island to prevent any land use other than limited forestry, restricted farming and 'primitive recreation.'" The Council's staff attorney, Catherine Johnson, was adamant that the use rights be taken and the owners not compensated (Arnold). This proposal, which was as unpopular as the earlier national-park proposal, seems to have gotten downsized and re-packaged as "Restore: the North Woods."

As defined on its official website, Restore is a proposal for a three-million-acre national park, the reintroduction of the eastern timber wolf, and the recovery and protection of wild forests in New England. Over its twenty-year quest for a national park, Restore has promoted itself as a charity and dismissed its opponents as profiteers.

As the new millennium arrived, Restore was no closer to its goal, and a wealthy environmentalist and a cofounder of Burt's Bees, Roxanne Quimby, engaged in a campaign to personally buy thousands of acres of Maine forest (much of which was former GNP land) and then donate it to the federal government for the purpose of starting a national park. Such a park would surely morph into the three-million-acre national park that Restore envisioned. I was in the room when Quimby was asked if she intended to grow her park beyond the initial seventy thousand acres. Her answer was no, because there were limits to the funding available for it. Just weeks later, she purchased another block of land. To illustrate what she thought of Maine residents, she once described Maine in an interview as a welfare state, and she tried to coerce Maine snowmobile clubs into supporting her park proposal for just five years of winter access across her land.

Quimby estimated that her park would attract approximately three hundred thousand tourists to the region. A fight quickly divided Millinocket over whether tourists would truly help the economy. The North Woods Park would allow primitive camping, not resorts, and it would be primarily seasonal; the economic impact, therefore, would provide little benefit to the community. A common fear that locals have regarding national parks is that they don't allow for local control and take away the ability of the locals to develop the land. They also fear environmental activists' constant push for buffer zones (protected areas near parks) and increased business regulations.

Not only do environmental activists try to engage in practices that prevent businesses that they deem undesirable from locating near parks, but the policies that they support also try to hamper existing businesses. In 2000, GNP, under the leadership of Lambert Bedard, was seeking financing for a complete remodeling of Millinocket's Number Eleven paper machine. The rebuilding required an emissions permit from the Maine Department of Environmental Protection (DEP). On July 28, 2000, the last day of public comment, the US Department of the Interior (DOI) sent a letter to the DEP expressing concern over emission changes and requested GNP to conduct the proper Class I assessments (Class I is a stricter air-quality measurement than the one required by DEP). Despite the fact that the Millinocket mill was more than one hundred kilometers (the statutory limit of control) from Acadia National Park and Moosehorn National Wildlife Refuge, the National Park Service (NPS) and the US Fish and Wildlife Service (FWS) sought to control emissions at the Millinocket mill (Bunyak and Silva).

The DEP issued the permit in August, and the DOI quickly appealed. It was operating under the Clean Air Act, which gives the managers of federal lands the responsibility of protecting the air quality within them and requires strict limits on pollutant increases within Class I areas. The complaint was that GNP didn't consult with the federal land managers (FLM) and that the DEP did not provide a valid analysis of the emission changes (State of Maine Board of Environmental Protection). The company enlisted the help of the town of Millinocket to lobby state leaders to find a quick resolution to the problem.

The requested tests were time-consuming, expensive, and unnecessary. The DOI's intervention delayed the final permit for several months. The delay caused the funding for the Number Eleven rebuilding to fall through. An alternative source of funding wasn't found, and Bedard got permission from the state of Maine to sell the massive hydro system to secure the necessary funding for the rebuilding (Conlogue). The sale of the dams permanently increased the cost of energy for the company and made it much more difficult for subsequent owners to maintain profitability.

Throughout the almost two decades of tragedy, the employment levels at the mill went from nearly four thousand to just over six hundred, before the Millinocket mill was shut down in 2008 (See figure five in Appendix A for a 2013 view of the Millinocket mill). By 2011, employment levels were around four hundred and the towns had lost thousands of residents because of the lack of work. In 2012, the East Millinocket mill employed only about two hundred fifty workers. Environmental activists could have claimed victory in their quest to restore northern Maine to pre-colonial status, but they didn't. As part of Governor LePage's negotiations to save the mills, he and the Maine legislature agreed that the state would assume liability for the mills' landfill. It was a surprising change of direction for a state whose policies were instrumental in the decimation of northern Maine's economy. There were numerous objections to the transfer of the liability for the landfill, but one of the more influential ones was from the Conservation Law Foundation, a liberal conservation group that claimed the transfer was unconstitutional. Fortunately enough, the group and its supporters didn't push the issue. But it was an unsettling distraction to a very delicate negotiation.

Another challenge from environmental forces came from Quimby, who seemed to pull forward her plans for a national park in northern Maine. I always felt that it was a strategic move that occurred just as Brookfield Asset Management was trying to sell the Millinocket and East

Millinocket mills. Industries are aware of the federal authorities' ability to regulate emissions and vistas (views) in national parks, and the threat of a national park could scare off some interested buyers. The political pressure increased about the same time Brookfield announced that if the mills were not sold, they would be torn down. Brookfield's tactic seemed to backfire, but the environmental pressure is still being applied.

For decades, the state seemed determined to encourage industry not to invest, and that is beyond all forms of common sense and sound financial planning. A company here, a company there, and pretty soon the state lost entire industries. The problem has been that the state seldom offers a plan to replace the lost tax base and jobs. Politicians will never be convinced that they are a primary cause of businesses leaving the state. But by making it more difficult to conduct normal business operations, they are doing just that.

Why would businesspeople tolerate being hassled simply for wanting to invest in their community? They wouldn't. No one would put up with a hassle if another state or country was willing to provide the same return on investment without the bureaucratic nightmare.

An answer to why businesses locate where they do can be found in these questions: Where do people shop? If consumers have two stores offering similar products at competitive prices, which one do they frequent? Do consumers shop at the store that is hard to get in and out of and has an inconvenient layout, or do they shop at the store that has easier parking and wider, more welcoming aisles and product displays?

Many of the foreign car companies that have assembly plants in the United States have located them in the South. Northern states tend to be more controlling and less willing to provide the necessary business climate to allow companies to flourish. One prominent Maine businessman told me that he purchased a business in Georgia, and when he met with the local code-enforcement officer, the officer said, "What can I do to make you want to invest in my town?" He said this was a complete 180-degree difference from what he found in Maine, where even a small objection in the initial stages of a plan can stop it before it even starts.

The enemies of Maine business spent forty years engaging in the politics of delay, divide, and denounce. The plan worked: the largest, most powerful, and wealthiest paper company in Maine was removed largely by these tactics. In his book, McCann argues that GNN decided not to make many necessary investments because of the high cost of doing business in Maine. Northern Maine's economy and environment, in the twenty-first century, is now much closer to what it was in 1800 than it was in 1900. Tom Griffin, speaking with great authority and knowledge of the region and paper industry said, "Remember, this did not have to happen."

The Future

The first obstacle in Millinocket's economic diversification in the past was its remote location. Second was a lack of developable land. The third obstacle was the attitude of the community; residents were still waiting for Great Northern to resurrect itself before they acted, and some of them were afraid of doing anything that would potentially offend whoever was the current owner of the mill. The fourth obstacle was the state of Maine; despite the tax benefits of "Pine Tree Zones" (the equivalent of urban enterprise zones), Maine remained a place where it was hard to procure business financing. It also remained hard to obtain permits for development, and even when permits are approved, they are sometimes challenged. The endless torrent of government bureaucrats that businesses have to please in order to procure the necessary permits keeps investment at bay.

A fifth obstacle relates to the town's attitude toward itself, of all things. A few years ago, town meetings, which were televised on local broadcast channels, became embarrassing displays of bickering that made the community the laughingstock of the state. The bickering and feuding between councilors provided scandalous headlines, hyping the feuds at the expense of the community. At the end of many of the published articles, one reporter would repeatedly point out the community's high level of unemployment and the town's distressed economy.

The town's internal bickering centered on competing visions for the future of the town. While all of the councilors wanted a better economy, some of the councilors felt that the town should be an inviting place for businesses, and others thought that the town should become a gateway community with the ultimate goal of having a national park. Some of the councilors realized that nature-based tourism doesn't generate enough taxable revenue to run a town, unless a major resort is the centerpiece. The public airing of these views divided the town and slowed any unity that could have moved the town in a positive direction. Negative publicity such as this is an obstacle to any business that may want to locate here.

It is like the case of the man who had a hot-dog stand in the city. He earned enough money to send his son to business school, and when the son graduated, he came home and said, "Dad, there is a depression on. People cannot afford hot dogs."

The father replied, "What's a depression?"

"That's when people don't have any money," the son replied. So the old man closed the hot-dog stand that put the son through college.

Despite the never-ending stream of bad news that seems to plague the Magic City, the community is not without opportunities. I wrote a piece for the local paper in 2002 pointing out how local housing could be used for economic development purposes. The thesis was that, with a 25 percent domicile vacancy rate and an infrastructure that could easily allow the population to double, it made perfect sense to promote the community to companies that had been spooked by 9/11 and were looking for a safe, stable place to locate strategic components of their businesses. It didn't happen; the houses were sold primarily to out-of-staters, who used them as vacation properties. At the time, many three-bedroom houses in the new developments, which were constructed from the mid-1950s to the mid-1970s, were selling for less than sixty thousand dollars, and two-bedroom houses went for around forty thousand. These properties represent an unbelievable opportunity for a company to locate here.

The Katahdin-Three's location, which is considered by most to be an obstacle, could actually be a benefit. The region is strategically located, and under the right circumstances, could become a distribution hub servicing Quebec, the Maritime Provinces, and northern New England. The local airport could facilitate the area becoming a hub. It was used extensively during WWII, because of its size and location. Furthermore, a private road (the Golden Road) already exists from Millinocket to Quebec. It needs upgrades before it could be used to transport consumer goods, but the key is that it is already in place. The Golden Road is only fifteen minutes from Interstate 95, further increasing the regions desirability.

Katahdin Timberlands selling the camp lots offers another potential long-term economic benefit to the community, because many banks will not lend money on leased land. By allowing personal ownership of the land, the camp lots are likely to incur more investment. These leases are located on land surrounding man-made lakes, lakes that were created by GNP's hydroelectric dams. The current owner of the dams, Great Lakes Hydro America (GLHA) (a Brookfield subsidiary), has maintained optimal water levels, which increases the desirability of the lakes. Furthermore, GLHA has the resources to properly maintain the facilities and is regularly performing needed maintenance. There are over one thousand seasonal properties to the west of Millinocket that contribute to a measureable increase in the Katahdin-Three's summer population. The seasonal increases could be key to attracting a retailer or other investment to the area.

There is hope for the Magic City, hope that comes from unexpected sources. For three seasons, the Pelletier family's *American Loggers* television show provided an immense amount of publicity. The Pelletiers' television success led to the creation of a trailer-manufacturing business, Pelletier Manufacturing, which specializes in manufacturing log trailers and truck-head boards. The *American Loggers* program illuminated values that made the Katahdin Region and America great: faith, hard work, and family. Americans have an interest in these virtues, and the economic activity that results is more lucrative than seasonal minimum-wage jobs that a national park would create.

Another economic opportunity for Millinocket resides in the form of urban decline in big cities. As cities are perceived as more and more dangerous and as terror threats become more frequent, smaller, rural communities have the potential to lure investment from companies whose employees are looking for a better, more cost-effective, higher-quality way of life. In the city, people pay hundreds of dollars a month for parking alone, not to mention the endless traffic jams. Many jobs could easily be done over the computer from the Magic City at a much lower cost and with a much higher level of productivity. The infrastructure is there, and the people are there. All that is necessary is for government to get out of the way and employers will recognize this and make magic happen once again.

Chapter Three

General Motors, The World's Largest Corporation

Readers may think that just because one community was devastated by the failure of a single company, it doesn't really mean that America's entire political and business systems are in a state of disrepair. But they are. I have another example of a company that started just one decade after Great Northern and became not only a leader in its industry but also the largest industrial corporation in the world. Like Great Northern, this company was initially the vision of one brilliant man who was said to have been able to put complicated stock swaps together in his head. The man's name was William C. Durant, and the company he started was General Motors.

General Motors (GM), Great Northern Paper (GNP), and their respective stories have a number of similarities. In the early part of the twentieth century, GNP claims to have had 40 percent of America's newsprint market (Great Northern Paper); in the 1950s, GM had 50 percent of America's automobile market. The history of GNP and GM is the history and future of America. These companies had the financial and intellectual resources to effectively innovate and compete, and they prospered as a result. The employees and communities that were associated with these giants prospered and epitomized the American dream.

When GM and GNP started to downsize, the American dream started to fade. When bankruptcy shrouded GM and GNP, the employees, communities, and investors were devastated. The jobs and tax base that disappeared have not returned.

The successes of GM and GNP, like the successes of most prosperous companies, are easier to chronicle because they had several key ingredients in common. These great companies started with a vision and a passion. The visions were allowed to develop because of capital. Through organization and innovation, the enterprises thrived. Finally, long-term success was facilitated with diversification and stability.

Vision and Passion

Entrepreneurs are like artists. They labor for a lifetime, growing and nurturing their creation. A business is an entrepreneur's canvas or clay. Every successful business has a founder with a vision and a passion to fulfill that vision. For GM it was William Durant.

The year was 1908. Henry Ford had just introduced the world to the Model T, and Durant was introducing the world to General Motors. Both men were self-made, but they differed completely in the skills that made them leaders in the automobile industry. Henry Ford, by far the more recognizable of the two, was an inventor who believed in a centralized business structure. Durant was a master salesman who believed in a decentralized structure. Though Durant did not bring a technical knowledge of the automobile to the industry, his contribution is no less significant than Ford's.

In his memoir *My Years with General Motors*, Alfred P. Sloan Jr., the former General Motors CEO, said that Durant came to the automobile business near the turn of the century via the wagon-and-coach-building business. In fact, he was the leading coachbuilder in the United States. In 1904, he joined the failing Buick Motor Company and reorganized it, and by 1908 Buick was the leading motorcar producer in the United States, with a production volume of 8,487 Buicks, compared with 6,181 for Ford and 2,380 for Cadillac (Sloan). Upon investing in the struggling Buick, Durant sought to raise working capital, so he focused his efforts on selling stock. He also set forth a reorganization of the company and increased production. When he went to the New York Auto Show in January 1905, he took orders with deposits far in excess of Buick's annual production. He also took a strategic long-term step by signing up dealers who had enough capital to purchase cars from the factory as they were produced (Wright). The first automobile company to join the "new" General Motors in 1908 was Buick, which was quickly followed by Olds a few months later. In 1909, Durant added Oakland (which later became Pontiac) and Cadillac. Sloan noted that each of the companies retained its corporate and independent operating identity, thus making General Motors somewhat of a holding company with independent satellite companies around it.

From 1908 to 1910, Durant brought some twenty-five companies to General Motors, over half of which were various manufacturers of parts and accessories. The companies were acquired through various means, but according to Sloan, stock swaps were the preferred method of acquisition.

Sloan said that Durant was "advanced for his time in his general methods of production" (Sloan). Durant believed in consolidation and felt that this could be accomplished through the extension of his product lines and through vertical integration.

Vertical integration, in a nutshell, means that the more stages of manufacturing a company undertakes in the production of a product, the more vertically integrated it is. If a company makes a product that requires ten subassemblies and it purchases all of the subassemblies from various suppliers, it is *not* vertically integrated. Vertical integration is a simple economic concept that is easy to explain but often difficult to implement. Unlike Durant, who already had Buick manufacturing some of its parts, many of the automobile manufacturers of that era assembled components that they had purchased from parts manufacturers.

In 1910, a cash-flow crisis prompted a consortium of bankers to force Durant out of GM's management in exchange for a loan (see the next section for more info on Durant's ouster). Due to the bankers' focus on efficiency and profitability rather than growth, GM's market share went from 21 percent to less than 10 percent by 1915. While GM was profitable in those years, it failed to match the growth seen in the rest of the industry (Pelfrey).

Durant was out, but he wasn't done. He immediately went to work building a new automotive empire, and by 1914 he had founded six more companies, one of which was Chevrolet. While he was forming his second automotive empire, he met a gentleman named John Jacob Raskob, a bookkeeper for Pierre du Pont. Raskob became an important ally of Durant's, and Raskob's connection to du Pont eventually saved GM.

Durant had also joined with Louis Chevrolet, a well-known race-car driver of the day, to produce a car to take on Ford. However, Chevrolet's vision was higher-performance cars, and Durant felt that the higher cost of such cars would render them less salable. Seeing what Henry Ford was doing with the low-priced Model T, Durant felt that the lower-priced segment offered the greatest opportunity. When Durant ordered a completely different version of the next-generation Chevrolets while Louis Chevrolet was in Europe in 1913, Chevrolet sold his one hundred shares of Chevrolet stock to Durant and left the enterprise (Pelfrey). Durant's vision, however, was correct, as Chevrolet sales soon skyrocketed.

While Durant was growing Chevrolet and the other companies, the bankers at GM ran the company in a very conservative manner. They searched diligently for the best people in an effort to bring in new talent. They reorganized operations and sold off unprofitable units. The bankers insisted that GM not pay dividends to shareholders until the loan was repaid, and this prompted some investors to sell their shares (Wright). Durant used the profits from Chevrolet to purchase the depressed GM shares, and by 1915 Durant and his allies, who included Pierre du Pont, had amassed a significant amount of GM stock (Pelfrey).

Durant ended up getting back on the board of directors, and he quickly enlisted a scheme to have Chevrolet, which was still independent, issue a new stock offering. The stock was quickly purchased by dealers and Durant's allies. The offering gave Durant the funds to purchase more GM stock. Durant held a Chevrolet stockholder's meeting to authorize an increase in capitalization to eighty million dollars (Wright). In this case, capitalization refers to the amount of stock that Chevrolet planned to issue, and with this extra stock, he made an offer to swap one GM share for five (later four) shares of Chevrolet (Pelfrey). Even Pierre du Pont bought into the offer, lending it a sense of legitimacy. By May 1916, Durant announced that Chevrolet owned outright 54.5 percent of General Motors stock, thereby giving Durant unquestionable control of GM once again.

After regaining control of GM in 1916, Durant formed United Motors Holding, a holding company made up of five manufacturers of parts and accessories. This company was rolled into GM in 1918. This proved to be a historic move, as it enabled GM to acquire two key people, namely Charles Kettering and Alfred P. Sloan Jr. (Wright). Kettering was an influential inventor, and Sloan would one day become chief executive officer and chairman.

The Need for Capital

The second ingredient that a successful business needs is capital or money. The best idea or product in the word is nothing unless the entrepreneur has sufficient capital to grow the business. GM's history is rich with examples of how sufficient and insufficient cash flows at different times caused major changes in the company.

In 1907, the country experienced a financial panic caused by a stock-market slide and the banks' resulting tightening of credit. The poor economy prompted many manufacturers to curtail production. Prior to the panic, Durant had secured sufficient amounts of financial capital before the stock-market slide, and therefore Buick was in a position to continue producing cars despite having to store some of them in warehouses. After the panic ended, Buick had a ready inventory of vehicles to sell, and when the dust settled, Durant had taken Buick from a failing company to the largest automobile producer in the country (Pelfrey). Durant seemed to have seen the panic coming, and so he made arrangements to acquire additional capital to tide the company over until the markets improved.

Durant was an ambitious optimist and a master salesman. He used these skills with brilliance and tact to form an empire. But not all of the investments paid off, and some of them actually were cash drains. Buick remained the star of the corporation, and much of the company's growth was based on the profits from Buick. When Buick's sales and profits fell in 1910, General Motors ran out of cash, and in an effort to save the company, it procured a loan from a group of banks. The bankers, in exchange for giving Durant a discounted fifteen million dollars, wanted him out of any management function. They also wanted their own people on the board of directors, GM to mortgage its physical properties, and six million dollars' worth of GM stock as a bonus (Wright). This was the background of Durant's first ouster from GM.

But his brilliance and vision allowed him to regain control of GM through Chevrolet in 1916 (as described earlier). The automobile industry was growing at a rapid pace, but World War I brought challenges to the industry. Investors feared that steel would be in short supply, and the price of GM stock fell. Pierre du Pont's assistant, John Raskob, in an effort to halt the slide of GM stock, urged du Pont to invest the company's wartime profits by purchasing GM stock on the open market. As a condition of the investment, Durant agreed that a finance committee controlled by du Pont's people would control the company's finances, while Durant continued to control operations through GM's executive committee (Wright).

The conclusion of the war brought about an economic boom, and in an effort to have production levels keep up with the increasing demand, Durant went on a buying spree, purchasing several companies based on their potential production capacity. In 1918, GM's sales were $270 million, and by 1919, they had risen to $510 million. On November 5, 1919, the finance committee in New York voted unanimously to accept a report showing estimated receipts and expenditures for a fifteen-month period ending December 31, 1920, and moved to raise as much as one hundred million dollars through the sale of debenture stock. The sale was authorized, but instead of raising the estimated eighty-five million dollars, it netted only eleven million, which was the first sign "that the corporation was in conflict with realities," according to Sloan.

The postwar years also brought about inflation. Sloan wrote that such inflation made budget overruns a regular occurrence, and that the weakness in GM's organization didn't become apparent until the effects of this inflation came to a head at the end of 1920.

In stark contrast to Durant, Henry Ford, who had taken his company private, generated capital for his company by reinvesting profits instead of issuing stock. Durant's buying binge and GM's lack of financial controls left GM in a delicate position, because the resulting market slowdown in 1920 reduced the ability of GM to raise capital via the stock market. Ford's different approach enabled it to ride out the storm and emerge stronger than ever (Pelfrey).

In late 1920, the country had entered a postwar recession, which had started to take its toll on sales. As with all recessions, the stock market began to slide—and with it, GM stock. Because of the unregulated growth in the previous years, GM was on shaky financial footing for the second time in ten years, and in an effort to support the price, a syndicate consisting of Durant, du Pont, Sloan, and others agreed to buy as much as ten million dollars' worth of GM shares on the open market. Durant was also buying on the open market independently, but he was buying on margins and paying as little as 10 percent (Wright). When GM stock continued to fall, brokers became nervous and began calling the margin. If Durant personally became insolvent, it would naturally reflect upon General Motors, and such an event could cause a panic.

When Durant brought this information to du Pont, Raskob, and Sloan, they devised a plan to form a holding company in which the du Pont interests would invest seven million dollars and a consortium of banks would loan twenty million. Durant's accounts would be paid from this money (Sloan). The bankers demanded Durant's resignation from the corporation, and this would be the last time Durant worked for the company he had founded (Seaman, "To Get Back in the Race…").

For the second time in just ten years, GM faced a major crisis resulting from a lack of cash. Having been a vice president during the crisis of 1920, Sloan said that by the end of that year, GM was compelled to borrow eighty-three million dollars from banks, and by 1922, it had to declare ninety million dollars in extraordinary write-offs, inventory adjustments, and liquidation losses (Sloan).

Durant was sixty-one in 1921, but instead of retiring, he started yet another automobile company, Durant Motors. One documentary on the stock-market crash of 1929 described Durant as a major stock-market speculator. Since most of his wealth was only on paper rather than in cash, he was hit hard when the market crashed. By 1933, Durant Motors was broke. In 1936, he filed for personal bankruptcy, claiming debts of over nine hundred thousand dollars and assets of two hundred and fifty dollars (basically, the suit on his back). Durant eventually opened a bowling alley in Flint, Michigan, and subsisted on a small pension provided by four of his longtime associates from GM, one of whom was Sloan (Wright). Sloan pointed out that, had Durant simply kept the remaining 230,000 shares of GM stock instead of selling his interest in the holding company that was set up to pay his debts, the value of the stock would have grown from $2.9 million to over $25 million (Sloan).

The Need for Organization

All businesses, organizations, and governments—regardless of their size, the brilliance of their leaders, and the amount of capital available to them—need to be organized. Durant was an innovator, and it was his constant innovation that enabled him to regain control of GM in 1916. It was Durant's lack of organization that led him to lose control again in 1920. Sloan wrote of Durant that he "was a great man with a great weakness—he could create but not administer." Sloan described Durant's failure to maintain control of GM as "a tragedy of American industrial history." The lack of organization leads to inefficiency, lower profits, and cash-flow problems.

When the restructuring of GM was complete in 1920, du Pont's interests owned over 40 percent of GM, and Pierre du Pont took over as chairman and president of General Motors. His first priority was to reorganize the mix of companies and divisions under the GM umbrella. He turned to Sloan, who had written an organizational study a year earlier. The plan applied the German staff-line concept to GM. The overall policies were to be developed by the central office. Carrying out the plans fell on the divisional managers, who were empowered to develop the specifics (Wright). Our founding fathers used a similar theory when forming our government. They envisioned a central government that set overall national policy yet at the same time gave the states the greatest amount of freedom so as to keep the power closest to the people.

This was just the beginning of Sloan's contributions to GM and the automobile industry. He became one of the most influential businessmen in the country. He was the first to apply the concepts of decentralization, strategy planning, and systematic organization to a large corporation. Under Sloan's leadership, GM's growth was unparalleled. Sloan instilled a culture of methodology, logic, results-oriented teamwork, and, most importantly, accountability (Pelfrey).

Sloan recognized that groups or committees can develop policies, but it takes individuals to administer them. A strident decentralizer, he lobbied for more power, not less, for the company's president. He felt that an individual, and not a group, should administer important policies, and that people needed an individual to turn to in the event of a crisis.

He increased the number of members on the executive committee, the highest committee in GM, in an effort to provide broader insight into operations, and he suggested the parameters by which they should operate. Sloan called his new management process "coordination by committee." He used his increased power to help coordinate the many divisions within GM. William Pelfrey, author of *Billy, Alfred, and General Motors,* summed up the decentralization-and-coordination concept as delegating decision making to operating divisions and field managers while at the same time holding them to clear and distinct performance objectives. Pelfrey went on to say that the Sloan model has become the litmus test for all kinds of organizations, and companies from all over the world have either implemented or borrowed from it.

One initial task concerned general purchasing. GM formed a General Purchasing Committee, which tried to realize economies of scale by purchasing in large quantities for all divisions. Sloan noted that the divisions resisted this move, but with their participation on the committee, they sought a balance between the divisions' autonomy and the corporation's overall interests (Sloan).

Next, GM looked to advertising. Sloan realized that with the exception of Wall Street, most people didn't know much about General Motors. He proposed forming the Institutional Advertising Committee, whose aim was to increase consumer awareness of the company.

The advertising campaign helped Sloan achieve what he felt was one of the biggest steps in "coordination"—that there should be more cooperation between the various divisions regarding engineering. In 1923, he recommended the formation of a General Technical Committee. The committee was to deal with general engineering problems of interest to the various divisions and to set broad engineering policies for the corporation (Sloan).

The General Technical Committee became the most powerful engineering advisory committee within GM. It developed standardized engineering policies, one of which was the development of GM's Milford Proving Grounds, an automobile-testing facility in Milford, Michigan. The controlled conditions within the proving grounds enabled standardized testing and comparisons between products. In the mid-1920s, the committee dealt with engineering problems concerning brakes, gas consumption, and lubrication.

Another key element in Sloan's reorganization of GM was his implementation of financial controls. He was vice president of GM in 1920 and didn't want to see GM ever threatened by cash shortages again. In his memoir, Sloan devoted a great deal of space to discussing the significance of proper financial controls.

One of the main problems during the Durant years was that each divisional manager received the maximum amount of capital requested without any effort on the part of the corporation to evaluate the proposal or to compare the amount requested with the amount of available funds. Sloan summed up the problem by pointing out three areas that exposed the weakness of the pre-1920 system: overruns on appropriations, runaway inventories, and a resulting cash shortage.

To help remedy the shortages in the prior appropriation process, Sloan and the executive committee enacted a set of rules to follow in evaluating proposed projects (Sloan):
1. Is the project a logical one, considered as a commercial venture?
2. Has the project been properly developed technically?
3. Does the project have the interest of the corporation as a whole?

4. What is the relative value of the project to the corporation as compared with other proposed projects?

The appropriation committee was to operate under the executive and finance committees, and the divisions were to make monthly reports of construction "in progress" to it. As Sloan wrote, "We were for the first time to get accurate and orderly information. After that it would be a matter of business judgment whether to grant a request."

The next area of attention was cash control. GM was critically short of cash in 1920 because, under Durant, it spent a lot of money growing the corporation without a proper strategic plan considering immediate needs. Prior to the changes, each division handled its own cash and paid its own bills, so the cash didn't flow through the corporation (Sloan). In 1922, GM set up a consolidated cash-control system, which, like many of the other controls, was the first of its kind for a large corporation (LaReau).

All deposits were to be placed in GM accounts that had been established in one hundred banks throughout the country, and all withdrawals were to be handled by the central financial staff and not the divisions. One of the benefits of the new cash-control system was that it increased the credit available to GM by establishing good working relationships with such a large number of banks (Sloan).

Sloan and his team also went to work instituting inventory and production controls. By creating set policies that required divisional heads to provide realistic sales estimates several months in advance and adjusting them as sales warranted, Sloan was able to better match GM's production with actual sales. By matching production to actual sales and matching inventories of parts to production, GM was able to significantly increase efficiency while maximizing cash on hand.

The most commonly recognized of Sloan's organizational achievements was a stair-stepped-price product portfolio. With seven car divisions in the early 1920s and no strategic plan from which to operate and market them, there was tremendous overlap in the product offerings. Sloan recommended creating a pricing structure that allowed each division to have a unique niche to operate without competing directly with the other GM divisions. Chevrolet led in the low-price field, followed by Oakland (Pontiac), Oldsmobile, Buick, and Cadillac as the luxury division.

This pricing structure was key to GM's establishing what is now known as a unique brand identity for each division. The successful establishment of separate identities for each division allowed each divisional manager to focus on the needs of specific customers and to tailor models to fit those needs.

The massive organizational restructuring that GM underwent in the 1920s was in itself a form of innovation. Many of the changes and policies had never been applied to a large corporation. They were so correct that they have become ingrained in the business curriculum as if they have always been part of the American enterprise system, but in the 1920s, they were an innovation (Pelfrey).

The Need for Innovation

Businesses need to have a willingness to constantly improve their products and systems—not simply changing for change's sake, but taking a good idea or product and making it better. Durant created a culture of product innovation within GM, and Sloan continued it.

Durant couldn't have been any more different from Ford. Whenever Model T sales were threatened, Ford's answer was to cut prices, whereas Durant continually improved his product, adding a starter and headlights as standard equipment. This wouldn't be the first time these ideologies would compete.

Due to the wildly ambitious and uncontrolled expansion under Durant's leadership, the early years of the GM story were immensely complicated. The lack of a formal organizational structure nearly caused the collapse of the company on two separate occasions. With a rational and respected du Pont in charge and Sloan at his side, GM was now setting the stage for decades of dominance of the auto industry. Sloan wrote in his memoir, "In 1921 Ford had about 60 percent of the total car and truck market in units, and Chevrolet had about 4 percent. With Ford in almost complete possession of the low-priced field, it would have been suicidal to compete with him head on. The strategy we devised was to take a bit from the top of his position conceived as a price class, and in this way build up Chevrolet volume on a profitable basis." Chevrolet and other GM products were changed and upgraded more frequently than Ford's Model T, and when people looked for a better vehicle, General Motors became the choice.

GM's General Technical Committee coordinated a host of innovations and advancements across all of its divisions. This led to the development of four-wheel brakes, "balloon" tires, and more. Sloan recalled that from 1924 to 1925, the General Technical Committee was providing information on the benefits of GM's engineering accomplishments to dealers and sales departments.

The development of a stair-stepped pricing structure and a coordinated engineering department enabled GM to perfect the model-year change. Sloan and Durant knew that the product had to be constantly improved and often changed to create a desire for consumers to purchase. Sloan felt that a car should last the average consumer four to five years under normal use. This would provide the best balance between the customers' value and the company's desire to maximize returns on investment.

The difference between GM and Ford couldn't have been more obvious. While Ford kept the Model T relatively unchanged from 1908 to 1927, GM constantly improved its cars not only mechanically but also in their styling. GM was, in fact, the first major company to create a styling department. Previous to that, the exteriors of cars were primarily designed by engineers.

This practice was to change forever; in 1926, GM under Sloan acquired the remaining interest in Fisher Body, making it a wholly owned subsidiary of GM. Sloan felt that a more pleasing design would sell better. The Fisher brothers told Sloan that they knew of a young designer in California who was doing some impressive work. The young designer's name was Harley Earl. He was put in charge of GM's newly-created color and design department. His first project was the 1927 LaSalle. The LaSalle was a lower-priced Cadillac that Sloan hoped would attract families that couldn't quite afford a regular Cadillac. In the end, it was so well designed that it made the more expensive Cadillacs look plain (Wright).

Earl believed in "dynamic obsolescence," or the notion that continuously improving the design of the car would create an urge in people to buy it. The divisions and the manufacturing department didn't like this, but Sloan also believed in it, and, as a result, the perfecting of the model-year change began (Wright). Earl's main design focus was to create beautiful and bold cars that always strove to be longer, lower, and wider than the ones they replaced. By the 1950s, Earl's designs were dominating the auto industry and influencing designs in other industries.

Another notable event in 1926 was the introduction of the Pontiac. Sloan realized that there was a gap large enough in GM's pricing structure between the Chevrolet and the Oldsmobile to allow a competitor to enter this high-volume segment of the market. His idea was to lengthen the Chevrolet body, use as many Chevrolet parts as possible, apply a different trim, and price the new car between the Chevrolet and

Oldsmobile (Sloan). The aim was to see if mass production could allow economies of scale on a variety of products instead of just one.

Sloan wanted to have the new car fall under the umbrella of the Oakland, which had been one of GM's weaker divisions, and priced between Buick and Oldsmobile. Chevrolet was to handle the development of the new car, and Oakland would provide the final trim and distribution. It was one of the first examples of coordinated planning and production involving several different divisions and departments. The eventual result was the Pontiac, and it was so popular that it eventually replaced its parent division, the Oakland.

Pontiac and the LaSalle were perhaps two of the first automobiles tailored to customers' needs and demographics, and not simply cars created with the hope that there would be a market for them once they are produced. GM was a leader in engineering advancements, and it finally had the exteriors to showcase these advancements. Sloan noted in his memoir that it took approximately two years to bring a car from concept to showroom. Ford's refusal to change and update the Model T cost him his sales leadership position in a mere seven years. GM's commitment to improving its products via engineering and styling had made it the largest automotive manufacturer in the world; it was a title the company would hold for over seventy years.

The Need for Diversification

Whether it's a business or a small community, there is a need for diversification so that the enterprise has multiple sources of revenue. This need becomes even more apparent in tough economic times. The cash shortages that resulted from declines in sales crippled GM during the Durant years. Proper integration of diverse assets in the 1920s enabled GM to emerge from the Great Depression stronger than many of its surviving competitors.

In 1918, Durant approached the inventor of the first electric refrigerator and bought the company that manufactured it (Guardian Frigerator Company, of Fort Wayne, Indiana). Durant then changed the company's name to Frigidaire, and he eventually sold it to GM for what he had paid for it. Durant didn't focus on just one thing, as Henry Ford did, and that dynamic culture continued under Sloan and his key advisors, Charles Kettering and Charles Wilson. Kettering was a prominent engineer and inventor. Wilson would eventually become GM's chief executive officer, and later President Eisenhower's secretary of defense.

General Motors, partly because of Durant's passion for growth, owned or held interests in several other companies that helped GM weather the economic storm of the Great Depression. The remnants of Durant's era included, but were not limited to, Frigidaire, GMAC, and Motors Insurance Company. The company eventually held interests in the aircraft industry and either owned or held interests in many other non-automotive businesses, including businesses in the railroad and radio industries. US automobile sales fell off a cliff and did not recover to 1929 levels for twenty years (Wright). But General Motors gained market share and remained a strong company because it had learned from previous crises how to control inventories and costs.

In 1932, during the low point of the Great Depression, the automotive units of GM lost money, but the nonautomotive units allowed GM to show an $8.3 million profit. It was a small profit, but the industry as a whole lost $125 million (Wright).

We must not forget the significance of the formation of General Motors Acceptance Corporation (GMAC) in 1919, and how its retail installment contracts made GM cars and trucks available to a much broader demographic. Basically, GMAC was a GM-owned private bank. And, as in the Depression era, much of the profits that GM earned in the early 2000s were generated from GMAC and not from GM's automotive divisions. The creation of GMAC also allowed dealers to finance their inventories, which enabled them to carry a larger selection of cars.

GM was now a global corporation with plants in Great Britain, Germany, and Australia. GM was a leader in pre-World War II Japan, but the country nationalized the GM plant in Osaka when the war broke out (Greimel). As a side note, nationalism and protectionist policies prevent GM from having a meaningful presence in Japan to this day. After the Pearl Harbor attack of December 7, 1941, GM, like all other domestic manufacturers, quickly turned from domestic automotive production to wartime military production. In a matter of months, GM was making critical components for the war effort. This quick shift enabled GM to produce various components, such as tank engines, aircraft parts, trucks, guns, and much more.

The Need for Stability

The financial crash of 2008 and the ensuing economic turmoil epitomize the need for a business to have stability. The federal government has injected over one trillion dollars in stimulus funding into the American economy in an effort to create jobs. News reports frequently state that American businesses are sitting on the largest amounts of cash that they have had in decades, but the businesses are not investing. Therefore, no jobs are being created. Occasionally, a business executive or financial manager will explain the lack of investment.

Business executives point to the amount of uncertainty emanating from the government. The federal government for four years, as of 2013, has not had a fiscal year budget, the Bush-era tax cuts have been extended for only short periods of time, and a bevy of new regulations has kept business only guessing. With no definitive spending, tax, or regulatory policies, businesses cannot make the necessary long-term financial commitments that would create jobs.

The financial crises of 1910 and 1920 had the same effect on GM. Durant's free spending and the country's economic problems caused instability within the investment community, and this was reflected in GM's stock price. Durant sold out for $9.55 per share on a Friday, and by Monday, with du Pont in charge, the price had climbed to $16.50 (Wright).

As president of General Motors, Pierre du Pont gave GM a much-needed level of credibility in the financial markets, not to mention a calming and stabilizing effect after the torrent of uncontrolled expansion under the Durant years. Pierre du Pont's mere presence as the head of GM helped to change the psychology of the whole corporation. The banks were reassured, the stockholders became more confident, and there was a renewed faith in the future of the organization. Pierre du Pont's administration gave the organization a sound structure from which to operate. Much of this was due to Sloan's organizational proposal, and when it came time for du Pont to step aside, in 1923, he nominated Sloan to be president of the corporation (Pelfrey).

Sloan's policies were designed to have a stabilizing effect by providing consistent policies, information, and returns on investment. Since Sloan knew the importance of the franchise system, in which the local dealers were experts in their own local markets, he put considerable resources into ordering the development of standard accounting procedures for dealers to follow and report to GM. This enabled GM to know the financial condition of each dealer in close to real time, and it helped GM maximize its operations for the betterment of the entire organization. GM also created Motors Holding in 1929. It financed qualified businesspeople who lacked the funds to purchase dealerships. These changes were another first—Ford and Chrysler didn't develop standardized dealer accounting and dealer-development programs for over twenty years (Teahen Jr.).

Sloan fully believed in the franchise system. In the early days, when the industry was in its infancy, a dealer's franchise could be terminated for any reason whatsoever, and another individual could be appointed. Inventory was often forced on dealers and left for them to dispose of the best way they knew how (Sloan).

Therefore, Sloan instituted an incentive policy that helped dealers alleviate some of the burden of disposing of unsold inventory. Sloan even had a railroad car outfitted as a mobile office, and he visited dealers throughout the country in an effort to hear dealer input, suggestions for products, and customer trends. In his memoir, Sloan finished the chapter on distribution by stating that there were problems that still needed to be resolved, and if they weren't, that could mean the end of the franchise system.

The alternative to franchising was either a system of factory-owned stores run by managers or a mechanism in which GM sold cars via a network of factory-authorized service centers. Sloan felt that neither of these alternatives was acceptable (Sloan).

In 1944, a seventy-year-old Sloan announced he would retire, and he proposed a succession plan. He handpicked Charles Wilson to be CEO, but the board of directors urged Sloan to stay on as chairman. Some felt that his presence had a stabilizing effect (Wright). When he finally retired, Sloan was eighty years old. GM had 50 percent market share and sixteen thousand loyal dealers.

Many books have been written about GM by brilliant people, chronicling all of its accomplishments throughout its one-hundred-year history. They talk about Earl's fabulous designs and about some of the people, in addition to Sloan, who made significant contributions to GM's success in the early years. These included Walter P. Chrysler, Charles Kettering, John Raskob, Henry Leland, Charles E. Wilson, Richard Grant, and Harlow Curtice. Then, after WWII, there was a new group of leaders who contributed to GM's legendary decades of dominance—men like Ed Cole, "Bunkie" Knudsen, Pete Estes, John Deloren, and Robert Stempel. Each of these men was a giant in his field. They all had enormous talent, and the Sloan system of corporate organization enabled each to fully utilize his talent and to propel GM to over 50 percent market share by the 1950s.

All of the innovations and great car designs speak for themselves. The people behind them also speak for themselves. It was Sloan's decentralization-and-coordination concept that allowed the talent to mature, just as wine has to mature to achieve its full potential. As stated before, General Motors was a decentralized corporation. Sloan and his team provided overall policy and coordination of resources for the various divisions, but the divisions were allowed autonomy to carry out the overall corporate plans. The general managers of the divisions were powerful, and they motivated the dealer network in ways that most books cannot capture.

Many of the greatest leaders that make up the GM story were engineers or had manufacturing backgrounds. When Ed Cole told Chevrolet dealers that Chevrolet was going to do something that required dealer help, they helped, because he had been Chevrolet's chief engineer and he was the father of not only the Cadillac V8 but also the legendary Chevrolet small-block V8. Most dealers, then and now, are shrewd businesspeople, and they know when they are talking to the real deal, someone who can get stuff done.

The vision and enthusiasm that Durant had used to start the corporation created a nucleus from which greatness would emerge. This greatness could not have been achieved without the methodical leadership of Alfred P. Sloan. His streamlining, organizing, and willingness to improve all aspects of the corporation created a lasting foundation without which GM could not have sustained its leadership position throughout so many years of mismanagement, hostile labor, and increased competition.

Chapter Four

Behind the Bankruptcy

H ow does the world's largest corporation go from dominating an industry to bankruptcy in one generation? Much has already been written about the subject, and much more will be written, but the long-term ramifications of the GM bankruptcy are still unknown. Just like the failure of Great Northern and the Magic City, GM's bankruptcy wasn't simply the result of a single event, person, or group. Rather, it was the culmination of many factors that spanned decades. It would take an entire series of books to catalog them all. I will simply try to present a detailed summary of some key items in an effort to provide an accurate picture of this tragic story.

Alfred Sloan

It almost seems that over the last decade, some people have tried to rewrite history, perhaps in an effort to shift the blame for GM's recent financial difficulties from latter-day missteps to, of all people, Alfred Sloan. The criticism of Sloan that I find the most disturbing is that—detrimentally, some say—he championed an accounting system that valued inventories as highly as cash. For those outside the automotive business, the basis of the criticism is that there are significant hidden costs associated with high inventories, such as storage costs, inventory taxes, and extra labor costs. While large inventories can be an Achilles' heel to a corporation, blaming Sloan or his accounting system for GM's (or any other corporation's) lack of profitability fifty years after he retired is absurd. It is the equivalent of blaming a drought on rain that used to fall.

Alfred P. Sloan was an innovator of efficiency. Had the infrastructure been in place to allow for "just in time" inventory systems to work in the United States prior to his retirement, he would have implemented them. The fact of the matter is, when Sloan stepped down as CEO of General Motors in 1946, at age seventy, personal computers hadn't been invented, nor had the interstate highway system been established. When he finally retired as chairman of the board in 1956, at age eighty, computers hadn't gained widespread acceptance, and the interstate highway system still wasn't complete. In a country the size of the United States, those two items are the key to such inventory-management practices. It is difficult to imagine being in charge of procuring hundreds of parts for assembly from scores of suppliers, to be delivered within a few-hour window to dozens of manufacturing facilities, without the aid of computers or the reliability of the interstate highway system?

Sloan's system was structured the way it was because there was no other way to manage an inventory system in the first half of the twentieth century. When technology allowed for increased efficiency and productivity, Sloan implemented it.

We have all heard the famous Henry Ford quote, "You can have any color you want as long as it is black." Well, during the early years of the automobile, manufacturers were using carriage paint, which was varnish-based. This type of paint didn't allow for as broad a range of colors as would be available later, and the reason they chose black was that it was less expensive and dried quicker. In his memoir, Sloan noted that it wasn't until an accident happened in 1920 at the DuPont laboratories that the company discovered a chemical reaction that allowed for a broader range of colors in a faster-drying paint. The paint would later be named Duco, a lacquer-based product, and after three years of joint research with GM, it was introduced in 1923. Author William Pelfrey listed Duco paint as one of many costly innovations that Ford resisted to his own detriment, because customers were willing to pay for them (Pelfrey).

The new paint had its problems. It sometimes peeled off the bodies, but Sloan felt that because of its overall benefits, it was worth the risk. One benefit was that it eliminated the need to store newly painted bodies for up to three weeks. At a production rate of one thousand cars per day, three weeks' production would require space for eighteen thousand cars in the production process. By eliminating this backlog of "drying" bodies, GM eliminated the need to have twenty acres of covered storage space in which to store them (Sloan).

I mentioned in the previous chapter that Sloan started the purchasing committee. This committee was the precursor to modern purchasing departments. He recognized the efficiency of having one unit purchase similar items in bulk, thus generating cost savings. He cited as the most important benefit the importance of standardization of parts and components. GM ordered the divisions to standardize parts wherever possible. Standardization eliminates the need to make an inventory of multiple components that serve the same purpose.

For those reasons alone, I feel that any criticism that lays the blame for GM's current problems on Sloan or the accounting system that he championed is misguided. But yet another reason he cannot be blamed is that Sloan was a master of return on investment. To illustrate the idea, he gave the example of a business that makes one hundred thousand dollars per year, operates at a profit, and is worthy of additional investment and increased capital because of superior returns on investment. He compared this business with another that earns ten million dollars per year and is unprofitable. This second business is unworthy of further expansion and may even require liquidation unless more profitable returns can be realized. The strategic goal of a business is to earn a return on capital, and if in the long run the returns remain unsatisfactory, the deficiency should be corrected or the activity abandoned for a more lucrative one (Sloan).

This last statement is the key to understanding the Sloan years at GM. Sloan studied engineering at the Massachusetts Institute of Technology, and many of the key people that moved up through the divisions and into senior management positions at GM had engineering or manufacturing backgrounds. This type of background lends a different view of problems than that of an executive with a background solely in finance. As a rule, finance people look to make an expensive operation or component cheaper, while an engineer looks at the same problem and tries to redesign it in an effort to make it more efficient and cost-effective.

There is a difference between cheaper and more cost-effective. *Cheaper* is what it is, but *more cost-effective* means the elimination of waste without sacrificing quality. This is a generalization, but the difference between the two can be subtle or extreme, depending on the situation.

Knowing who is not to blame for the recent General Motors debacle does give us a starting point from which to make an analysis of where responsibility does lie. The retirement of Alfred P. Sloan from GM didn't mark the beginning of the end for GM; it simply marked the end of the beginning. There was still a brilliant management team in place with the ability to fully utilize their skills in the decentralized structure that Sloan established. They continued the annual styling changes that Sloan and Earl had long championed, and GM continued to earn great returns on its investments.

There are a lot of places to put blame for the GM bankruptcy. I have been watching this closely for the better part of two decades. In fact, when I was a senior in college, a group of us were assigned to give a re-port on the world automobile market. The group consisted of a student from Japan, three students whose families had small businesses, and the class valedictorian. Years before the automotive bankruptcies, we discov-ered that GM, Ford, and Chrysler were operating with significant cost disadvantages, because of onerous union contracts and high health-care costs. We also noticed that the domestic automobile manufactures made significant improvements in quality, but hadn't improved the perceived quality gap with import manufactures.

I have seen bits and pieces presented on this subject, but I would like to present what I feel are the key causes of one of the largest bankruptcy cases in US history. These are not in any particular order, nor are they the only causes. Earlier in the book, we found that labor unions, the government, and management formed a trio of destruction for Great Northern Paper Company and Millinocket. These three are just as rel-evant to the GM example, but to them we have to add two more: distri-bution (or dealers) and the media.

Labor vs. Management

The tension that exists between many employees and their employ-ers is a troubling issue. Employers need the employees as much as the employees need the employers. The labor unrest at Great Northern and

General Motors made little sense to outsiders. After employees got safe working conditions and better-than-average pay (in the case of GNP, the workers also respected management), the influence of the unions should have waned. At the peak of the labor unrest and for many years after, the compensation packages contributed to the companies' lack of competitiveness.

While the 1978 strike at GNP was in large part instigated by a conflict between the trades and papermakers' unions, a significant part of labor unrest, in general (especially at GM), may be attributed to a conflict between the businesses' and employees' respective views of rewards. For decades, businesses have tried to operate at a point where the marginal (additional) revenue (MR) from the sale of an additional unit is equal to the marginal cost (MC) to produce that unit (MR=MC). This is a basic law of business and is taught to all college business students.

The MR=MC formula is affected by two other laws of business: the Law of Declining Marginal Utility and the Law of Diminishing Returns. Retired Husson University professor Phil Grant, PhD, summarized the Law of Declining Marginal Utility by stating that a business has to charge less per unit to sell more, because additional units consumed produce less and less utility or value per unit. The Law of Diminishing Returns says that costs to produce additional units increase at an increasing rate as volume increases, because additional units of input (i.e., additional amounts of labor) produce less and less marginal output.

In an effort to more accurately reflect the effects of employees into the business formula, Dr. Grant developed the Effort-Net Return Model of employee motivation/satisfaction, which states that an employee will produce at a point where the perceived marginal reward equals the marginal sacrifice (additional personal cost), because this is the point where the employee maximizes his or her personal satisfaction. The key to the Effort-Net Return Model is the Law of Escalating Marginal Sacrifice. According to Dr. Grant, as employees increase effort to accomplish a task, they perceive that they will incur greater personal costs such as fatigue and stress (Grant). These perceived costs increase at an increasing rate as the individual approaches his or her effort capacity, similar to the cost function in the Law of Diminishing Returns.

Dr. Grant's mathematical proof shows that "company volume is in large part determined by the slope (rate of change) of the company incentive function (incentives are a cost to the company and a reward for the employee) and the slope of the employee sacrifice function. It is where the slopes of these two functions are equal that determines volume—not where the slopes of revenue and company cost are equal (not where MR = MC)" (Grant). Therefore, a company maximizes profit at a point before MR=MC.

The application of Dr. Grant's work could potentially help improve labor and management relations. The 2010 nursing strike at Eastern Maine Medical Center (EMMC) is a recent example of labor relations that could be explained by Dr. Grant's research. The nurses went on strike not because of wages or benefits but because of a difference of opinion on staffing levels. Nurses are well compensated, and the union knew that it couldn't win a public-relations battle if it went on strike over wages, but if the strike was over low nurse-staffing levels, which pose a public-health safety risk, it might win the argument. I am not saying the nurses were wrong, but basically the nurses were saying that while they agreed with their compensation (reward), they viewed their sacrifice (personal cost) as being too high. Their perceived sacrifice curve was higher than the incentive curve.

This helps to explain why, despite compensation being higher than for non-unionized automotive jobs, perceived UAW labor sacrifices trumped the goals of GM and the other domestic auto manufacturers. I'm not saying that the employees were not worth the compensation that they received, but I do feel that unsustainable compensation packages combined with stringent work rules created an atmosphere that contributed to the Big Three automakers' not being competitive.

The Unions

Naturally, there will be some who will criticize me and say this is the second time in just a few chapters that I'm picking on the poor, defenseless unions, but the United Auto Workers union was an instrumental player in this saga. The original United Auto Workers (UAW) contract with GM in 1937 was a one-page document (Jackson, "Bitter Strike Gave Birth…"). The contracts that were to follow became increasingly complicated and costly.

I remember Ron Gettelfinger, the president of the UAW, talking in December 2008, when GM and Chrysler were in Washington, DC, pleading for money. Gettelfinger said that if union members worked for free, it wouldn't help; they comprise only 10 percent of the cost of a car. He is good at portraying the union as an innocent bystander in this story, but when comparing the wages of a UAW worker at GM with that of a non-union worker at Toyota, there was a significant difference in compensation.

In 2005, the average labor costs per hourly worker in the United States reported by GM and Toyota were $73.73 and $48, respectively. It is important to note that these figures are all-inclusive—they include hourly wages, retirement costs, and health-care costs (Geng). Toyota doesn't provide a pension like GM, nor does it provide retirement health insurance like GM did. GM's health-care cost per car in 2004 was $1,525, compared with $201 for Toyota (Geng). Considering the amount of time it takes GM on average to assemble a vehicle compared with Toyota, and factoring in the average labor cost for each, GM incurred a $1,200 to $1,300 greater labor cost per vehicle. Worth noting is the landmark labor agreement of 2007, which lowered labor costs and shifted the health-care burden to a union-operated trust. Steven Rattner, the head of President Obama's automotive task force, said that by the time of the bankruptcy, GM had almost equaled Toyota's labor costs and assembly productivity (Rattner).

It is important to recognize how the union arrived at the disproportionate compensation packages that were prevalent in the pre-bankruptcy years. The following discussion will reveal several other factors outlining why the union is at least partially responsible for the bankruptcy.

Sloan dedicated a whole chapter in his memoir to labor relations. The unions had long tried to break into GM and organize the workers. Their strength was finally used as a weapon in 1936 and 1937, when the union organized sit-down strikes. Sloan described them as "strikers who had seized our property," and he urged the governor of Michigan and even President Roosevelt to intervene and help negotiate a solution, but they refused (Sloan).

Roosevelt and the governor urged GM to negotiate on its own with the union, thereby giving the union a greater degree of legitimacy. It is easy to relate to a homeowner or small-business owner who is illegally locked out of his or her property by a third person. It is more difficult to accurately relate to the frustration that would occur if, when the property owner approached the local authorities, all the authorities said was, "You should negotiate a solution with the squatter." In the GM case, the actions of the government (or the lack thereof) amounted to anointing the union as the "chosen ones." The strike, which started at one of the Fisher Body plants, eventually caused GM to shut down its assembly plants, because there were no cars being produced. Sloan felt that the sit-down strikes were patently illegal, and the US Supreme Court eventually agreed, but the damage was done (Sloan).

During WWII, the country was unified and the federal Wage and Labor Law provided some stability insofar as labor relations were concerned. But the guns had barely cooled when the UAW staged a 119-day strike from late 1945 to early 1946. The UAW was one of the largest unions in the country and wasn't afraid to flex its political muscle. Sloan believed that many of the union spokesmen were "hostile to private enterprise," and the apparent result was to compete with each other "in a show of 'militance' against the corporation" (Sloan). Much of this animosity against the corporation perhaps derived from a Communist element within the UAW; Sloan noted that labor relations improved when the Communist element was defeated and discredited in 1948.

Concerning this and other strikes, Sloan wrote, "It appeared that the UAW was able to enlist the support of the government in any great crisis." He felt that President Truman prolonged the 1945–46 strike by formally backing the unions' demands that wage increases be based on GM's ability to pay. Even remote communities like the Magic City were unable to escape the national unions' antagonistic arguments. The problem with the "you can afford it" argument is that what can easily be paid today may be hard to pay tomorrow.

By 1948, the union had moved beyond asking for a better wage and began asking for more benefits. The employee benefits, which were established in those years and throughout the subsequent decades, were a factor behind GM's lack of wage competitiveness. As a point to ponder, Rick Wagoner, GM's chairman from 2000 to 2009, testified to Congress in 2008 that over the previous fifteen years, GM had spent $103 billion on pensions and retiree health-care obligations alone (Frick).

Until recently, another seldom mentioned component of the union contracts was job banks. Job banks are a pool of laid-off workers who receive about 90 percent of their pay for up to two years after being furloughed. These workers are placed on hold in case they are needed at a plant at some future time. The union agreed as part of the new labor contract to eliminate this practice, but while it was in effect, the cost to fund it was in the millions. The end result was that these job banks led GM, Ford, and Chrysler to treat labor expenses as a fixed cost rather than a variable cost. In most businesses, labor is a variable expense, and if you produce less, that expense goes down. The job banks didn't allow that. Therefore, the manufacturers had an incentive to build as many cars as possible to reduce the average cost per car (Rattner). The overproduction caused many problems, one of which was that the automakers came to depend on high rebates, which cheapened the value of the brand.

I've briefly shown several of the results of GM's labor agreements with the union that kept the company from being a cost-competitive producer. But the costs are not the whole story. Labor agreements don't always deal with benefits and wages. Sometimes labor agreements have caveats, such as the "neutrality agreement," or a guarantee of product plans allocated to specific plants.

For example, the latest agreement that was reached as a result of the bankruptcy specified that the new Chevy Volt and another small car would be produced in the United States and not in China or Mexico. Unions have long demanded that jobs stay in the country. The UAW's 1976 contract stipulated that GM should not discourage or encourage employees in the plants from joining the UAW. The "neutrality agreement," as it became known, derived from the union's accusations that GM was implementing a southern strategy. The southern strategy was, according to the union, GM's effort to relocate plants to the South, where labor was cheaper and unions were weaker. The unions pressured GM to keep jobs in the union-friendly North (Sorge).

To illustrate the animosity that the unions held, one GM dealer described a group tour of an assembly plant in the 1970s. As the tour started, the GM executive who led the walkabout gave the dealers strict instructions not to say anything to any of the assembly-line workers. He said if they saw workers forget to tighten a bolt, they shouldn't say anything to them; if they did, the crew would shut down the line. He went on to say, "Tell us, and we will make a note to catch it in the inspection." It was a contract year, and he said the unions were looking for any excuse to shut down a line.

The unions continually used strikes as a weapon, trying to strike at the jugular of the corporation, though the corporation was a necessary part of the symbiotic employer/employee relationship. The unions also held national strikes in 1970 and 2007.

The 1970 strike was yet another bitter strike that had far-reaching implications. One dealer told me that it was ninety days before his dealership received a new car. By the time the strike ended, he said he was down to just one new car, a Pontiac T37. During that strike, the shipment of parts was also interrupted, thus significantly reducing the revenue that the dealership derived from the mechanical shops. The dealer believed in taking care of his team, and he refused to lay off any workers, though he didn't have any new cars to sell, had fewer used cars ("program cars" were not available during those years), and had fewer mechanical repairs, due to a lack of parts. The local Ford dealer even approached him and said, "I wish those guys would get back to work, this is hurting our sales too." The GM dealer said that as soon as the strike was over, his employees all came in and demanded a raise. The unions' example and actions disrupted the entire country and set the stage for an unnecessary amount of widespread employee/employer tension.

According to Marjorie Sorge of *Automotive News*, some of the provisions in the contract that got the 1970 strikers back to work were: there would be unlimited cost-of-living increases, to be adjusted annually for the first two years and quarterly for the third; GM would pay all of the health-care premium increases; and GM would pay a five-hundred-dollar-per-month pension for workers who were fifty-eight years old with thirty years of service. She also mentioned that the strike was costly not only to GM, which lost millions in sales, but also to the union: "The UAW's strike fund went broke and it had to borrow $25 million from the Teamsters, $10 million from the Steelworkers, $121,000 from its locals, and $11.5 million from banks."

The 2007 strike was only a few days long, and it was more of an effort to mitigate concessions than to bleed the company. The unions did, however, agree to a major deal that was to eventually shift the monstrous fifty-one-billion-dollar burden in retiree health-care liability from GM to a union-managed trust called the Voluntary Employee Beneficiary Association (VEBA). GM was to pay the union more than thirty-six billion dollars over several years to fund the program (Healey and Carty). The benefits of the 2007 labor agreement were to give GM near parity with the "transplant" manufacturers.

Unfortunately, it was too little too late. Decades of burdensome work rules and above-average compensation levels added to the demise of one of the world's largest corporations. I was surprised when I did some searches on the Internet and found references to UAW contracts weighing twenty-two pounds. No company can withstand a burden like this forever. It may sound ironic, but excessive employee compensation and labor rules will eventually lead to a decline in the employees' situation.

In her *Automotive News* article, Sorge quoted Sloan's concerns about GM unionizing. He wrote:

What made the prospect seem especially grim in those early years was the persistent union attempt to invade basic management prerogatives. Our rights to determine production schedules, to set work standards, and to discipline workers were suddenly called into question. Add to this the recurrent tendency of the union to inject itself into pricing policy and it is easy to understand why it seemed, to some corporate officials, as though the union might one day be virtually in control of our operation.

Sloan's ability to look so far into the future is lacking in modern corporate America. Not only would the union increase its influence within the corporation, but it, with the help of the US government, would also become the second-largest shareholder of GM. One can only hope that with the increased stake that the UAW holds, labor relations will continue to improve for the betterment of the nation.

I don't begrudge the unions' trying to better their members' quality of life and standard of living, but at some point, it seemed to become an "anti-management" type of vendetta. It wasn't all the workers who felt this way, and the bankruptcy wasn't entirely the union's fault. In the early years of the labor movement, working conditions were abhorrent and there were no protections for workers. Through tough negotiations, working conditions, wages, and protections were all dramatically improved. However, at some point, demands became unreasonable and unsustainable.

Determining when workers' compensation becomes unreasonable is a delicate balancing act. Compensation has to be high enough for the employee to make a living, but cost-effective enough for the employer to be able to afford it. What is reasonable and affordable in one market cycle may be oppressive in another. One real example (from the old GNP) of unreasonable work rules and compensation is an employee (a pipe fitter, for example) who has to call an electrician to replace a light bulb that has burned out. Another example is that if an employee is called in for a problem after his or her normal workday has ended, the employee is entitled to six hours' pay even if he or she is only there for twenty minutes. If the employee goes home, the problem resurfaces, and the employee is called back in, he or she is entitled to another six hours of pay.

The danger of unsustainable compensation packages is that even in bad years when the company should be reinvesting in the operation, it is forced by a pre-negotiated contract to increase wages or benefits. A compensation increase in the middle of a recession could make the difference between a capital investment paying off or being considered a loser.

The power of unions has weakened considerably in recent years, but the unions couldn't have gotten as powerful as they became unless they had help.

The Government

By openly supporting the unions during strikes, politicians, in a way, handpicked the winner. This favoritism can be traced to the 1937 sit-down strike, when Sloan said that President Roosevelt and Michigan Governor Frank Murphy had openly urged GM to negotiate with the lawbreakers who had seized its plants and shut down production rather than using the police or National Guard to enforce the law. This continued until GM finally felt obligated to negotiate to regain control of its plants.

Sloan also said that President Truman openly agreed with the unions' charge that the contracts should be based on GM's "ability to pay" (Sloan). But just because it can, it doesn't mean it should. The unions championed a system where everyone got an equal share of the corporation, and the government seemed to fall hook, line, and sinker for it. The philosophy that the unions espoused appears to be inspired by Karl Marx.

Marx's philosophy maintained that people should be paid "from each according to his ability, to each according to his need." US politicians will never openly admit to following the teachings of Karl Marx, but their actions and words often tell a different story. As I have said before, initially the unions were a good influence on business, but eventually they became burdensome. Government meddling in the union/corporation relationship skewed the power in favor of the unions. Everyone prospered for several decades, but, in a global marketplace, decades of delayed investment, partially the result of unsustainable compensation packages, has caused workers and small towns to severely suffer.

I suppose one could liken it to having an ice-cold beer on a hot summer day. One tastes good, two is better, and the next thing that happens is someone is making a beer run on a riding lawn mower, because his wife took away the car keys. The next day, if he chooses to sober up, the beer drinker has to deal with a hangover and an angry wife. Choosing to do this long enough may cause cirrhosis of the liver and a broken marriage. The unions' contracts were so good that the hangover helped to kill the patient. The government in this story was the one supplying the beer—the enabler.

It took several years to see the full effects, but one of the side effects of these contracts was that they added fuel to the inflation fire of the seventies. When GM and the unions agreed to a wage formula proposed by GM in 1948, some experts criticized the plan because they felt that it could create an inflation spiral. The plan, in part, provided an annual pay raise based on the cost of living and an "improvement factor." The improvement factor was to be based on increased productivity. The problem with the latter is that it is hard to measure increased worker productivity, because much of the improvement is the result of capital improvements that make the worker more efficient. Sloan agreed with the assertion of Charles Wilson, president of GM at the time, that GM's wage policy did little more than protect its employees from inflation. Sloan did mention that experts had also criticized the benefit packages for the same reason (Sloan).

The cost of the benefits rises with inflation, and the company has to absorb the cost, thereby creating inflationary pressure when combined with wages. The unions didn't create the inflation, but these contracts added to it. The government's reaction to the inflation situation didn't address all the problems. Some might say that the federal government actually made inflation worse through misguided policies.

Federal, state, and local governments are all guilty of creating policies that restrict a business's ability to freely interact with its workforce. Union favoritism, in an effort to garner votes or endorsements, is a part of this. What the government doesn't realize is that labor contracts, which are often written in boom years, call for specific pay increases and fixed benefits must to be honored in the lean years that always follow. When a business like General Motors is forced, partially by political pressure, to sign a labor agreement that is excessive, it often has to forgo necessary capital improvements and research and development, putting it at a competitive disadvantage when the economy improves.

Pusillanimous politicians, who constantly pander for votes and persistently vilify corporations, have created an environment in which even quality, civic-minded corporations are viewed as immoral greedsters. In some ways, the incessant badgering from government, in the form of ever-increasing and changing regulations, force many companies into becoming greedster-like. Increased regulations add tremendous cost to operating a business. How can a company look five or ten years forward with a government that is constantly moving the target?

All companies that make automobiles have to abide by the same fuel-mileage standards, emission requirements, and safety standards. But companies that assemble automobiles in other countries, especially in developing economies, don't have to abide by the same labor laws, environmental laws, and regulations. In many instances, these regulations alone place American companies at a global disadvantage, and when our legal system is factored into the mix, the disadvantage becomes even more obvious.

In his 1992 book *Agenda for American Renewal*, President George H.W. Bush said that, over the previous thirty years, federal lawsuits had almost tripled. He went on to state that our civil justice system was "slow, expensive, and putting us at a global disadvantage." The verdicts and damage awards issued by juries and activist judges force American companies like General Motors to pass on the costs to consumers in the form of higher prices. It isn't just the cars but insurance and health care that become more expensive. The entire manufacturing community is forced to deal with higher operation costs as a result.

Just to put these costs in perspective, President Bush cited a study by the National Association of Manufacturers that said Americans spent as much as two hundred billion dollars a year on fees to lawyers. That figure didn't even include money paid to lawyers on corporate payrolls or money spent on court settlements. He also noted that foreign companies spent only 6 percent of the product-liability insurance US firms carry. Those numbers are from 1992, and the legal pandemic has only gotten worse.

An offshoot of poor government regulatory policies is the health-care system. Prior to the bankruptcy, General Motors spent on the order of $1,500 per vehicle in health-care costs (Will). GM had one million people on its health-care rolls, at a total cost of $4.6 billion (Jackson, "Health care: From…"). The Affordable Care Act (Obamacare) notwithstanding, The United States is the only major industrial country in the world that doesn't have a national health-care system. I'm not advocating for a national health-care system, but I am saying that GM's health-care burden was instrumental in its bankruptcy. Regardless of the lack of a universal health-care system, the fact remains that the US government has instituted policies like Obamacare that make it almost impossible for American companies to compete on a level playing field with much of the world.

Burdensome regulations increase costs, reduce international competitiveness, and enslave businesses to the whims of a fickle political system. Tax policies on a federal basis can give one country an advantage over another. Even the taxation policies of state and local governments can create competitive disparities.

Traditionally, most of GM's automobile manufacturing facilities were concentrated in the Midwestern states. These states, in an effort to sustain their tax base, naturally supported the unions' efforts to keep auto production located there rather than in the South, where the companies would have enjoyed significant cost savings.

Government policies don't simply affect a corporation's tax obligations; they also often increase costs in ways that are frequently overlooked by reporters. I remember listening to the debates in Congress when the government started to deregulate utility companies. Senator Trent Lott of Mississippi said that electric companies (southern utility companies) had competitive advantages and intended to keep them. By design, manufacturing companies, especially those engaged in the production of automobiles, are immense consumers of electricity. A few pennies per kilowatt can add or subtract vast sums from the bottom line of a large manufacturer like GM. Rather than creating an "American solution" to that particular problem, Senator Lott simply looked to continue his region's advantage over other parts of the country. Perhaps if those in the US government were more focused on what is best for America and less focused on being lifelong bureaucrats with generous pay and benefit packages, we wouldn't be dealing with the export of millions of US jobs and the bankruptcy of GM.

It almost seems as if there is an undercurrent in this country, a segment that wishes to sabotage icons of capitalism like General Motors. It is either that or gross incompetence on the part of our elected/appointed leaders. Our country has promulgated policies that have significantly increased operating costs for businesses of all types, from the smallest mom-and-pop store to large manufacturers. The government, through bureaucratic agencies that interpret these regulations, has also acted as an impediment to business development and growth. Occasionally, when the businesses are having a hard time, someone will propose a change in an unpopular policy or a small tax reduction in an effort to guarantee him or her reelection. Then, almost as if it was a coordinated effort, our government grants a country like China "most-favored nation" status or passes a treaty such as NAFTA, giving these countries virtually unfettered access to our markets. US companies like GM are under tremendous burdens with expensive union contracts and government regulations and are often forced into bankruptcy or to relocate operations overseas in an effort to compete.

This has been going on for decades. Americans should remember the giant sucking sound that Ross Perot spoke of in his 1992 bid for the presidency. In 1993, *Ward's Automotive Yearbook* reported figures from the US Bureau of Labor Statistics that showed the average wage that a Mexican autoworker earned in 1991 was $3.33 per hour. A Korean autoworker made only $6.42 per hour, compared with $24.21 per hour paid to the average UAW worker (as cited in Thompson and Strickland). Not only did these developing countries have wages that were many times lower than those in the United States, but they didn't have to abide by the same labor and environmental laws nor with the same health-care costs. At times, these countries also had currency-exchange rates that were a significant competitive advantage.

In the 1970s, the government, in response to the 1973 Arab oil embargo, imposed fuel-economy standards for automobiles sold in the United States. Instead of imposing a gradual increase in the federal fuel tax, as the Europeans did, the US government chose to mandate the Corporate Average Fuel Economy (CAFE) standards. A gradual increase in the fuel tax would have increased the cost of gasoline and the consumer would have naturally considered more fuel-efficient vehicles, as did the European consumers (Lutz, 2011). Instead, auto-mobile manufacturers were required immediately to meet stringent fuel-economy standards. The Japanese manufacturers, because they had already dealt with high fuel costs and more congested cities, more than met the standards. Therefore, the Japanese had the chance to gradually increase the size and comfort of their already fuel-efficient cars to appeal to a broader spectrum of Americans. The Europeans were in a similar situation. Unfortunately for American manufacturers, their cars had to be radically downsized and lightened to improve fuel mileage (Lutz, 2011).

The downsizing required an enormous amount of engineering to achieve. This was happening at the same time that the automak-ers were working to improve vehicle-emissions standards. The addition of numerous antipollution devices further complicated the process. GM switched from making full-framed, rear-wheel-drive cars to mak-ing unibody (in which unitized construction integrates the vehicle's frame or safety cage into the body of the car, thus saving weight), front-wheel-drive cars that were much smaller and lighter than the cars they replaced.

GM, which was the strongest of the Big Three manufacturers, was able to lumber through the process, while Chrysler almost went bank-rupt and Ford struggled. But GM did suffer massive problems. The quick onset of the new designs required all-new engines, transmissions, and drive systems, in addition to the all-new body architectures. Vehicle problems increased at a point in time when some (not all) imports of-fered more reliable alternatives.

Retired GM vice chairman Bob Lutz said, "From the smallest Chevrolet to the largest (but now smaller) Cadillac, every part in every car was new! When that much change occurs in such a short time, the probability of error grows exponentially, and these hastily-conceived cars were rife with problems, destroying in two to three years a reputation for industry-leading quality that had been built over decades" (Lutz, 2011). Not all of the products were bad, just as not all of the imports were good, but it soured public opinion and it gave the media ammunition.

The Media

GM's struggles with quality in the 1970s and early 1980s came at a time when the book *Unsafe at Any Speed*, by the consumer advocate Ralph Nader, was fresh in the minds of the American public and an ambitious media. If asked when General Motors started to decline, many people might point to the Chevrolet Corvair. They will most likely cite *Unsafe at Any Speed* as proof that GM was neglecting the well-being of its customers. Just as Bob Woodward and Carl Bernstein inspired a generation of political journalists, the success of Nader and his book inspired a generation of automotive journalists.

This book was perhaps one of the first publications that attacked the American automobile industry head-on. With the success of Nader's book, vilifying GM and other American manufacturers became a common occurrence. Publishing or broadcasting what would sell and not necessarily what told the "rest of the story," as Paul Harvey would say, seemed to become an acceptable practice for some outlets.

Nader's book criticized the entire American automobile industry, but the Corvair became the example. Nader used trial transcripts that showed that GM didn't properly inform dealers and the public about the car's specific tire-pressure recommendations and driving characteristics. The book also showed that GM encouraged dealers to order optional springs and stabilizers, which helped the car's handling. He went on to illustrate the American automotive system that allowed design problems to linger longer than they should, that made cars that polluted more than they should, and that lacked basic safety equipment (Nader).

For many Chevrolet dealers, one of the biggest customer-satisfaction problems the Corvair exhibited was that its air-cooled aluminum engine leaked oil. Sometimes the oil dripped onto the manifold, and the resulting oil smell would enter the car through the manifold heater. The oil also ended up as an unsightly film on the car's rear grille. It wasn't until many years later that seals were developed that were able to correct this problem. Nader and other critics claimed that because of the poor design of the rear suspension, under hard corner maneuvers, the rear wheel would roll under the car. An interesting note often left out of the debate is that Porsche used a similar suspension design. By the time Nader's book came out, Chevrolet had installed heavier springs and stabilizer bars to mitigate the problem.

As Nader stated in his book, some of the Corvair story involved a communication problem. Chevrolet recommended that fifteen pounds of air be put in the front tires and twenty-six pounds in the rear. That was a key component that allowed the car to handle properly at highway speeds. When customers took their cars to a service station, the attendants would often air up all four of the tires to thirty-two pounds. The handling problems could often be attributed to incorrect air pressure. In a 2011 film commemorating Chevrolet's one hundredth anniversary, GM cited actual collision statistics that showed that real-world Corvair statistics didn't vary much from those of other makes of the era (Chevrolet Motor Division).

The Corvair did introduce several rather progressive advancements. First, it was an air-cooled, rear-drive, rear-engine design. The car was incredibly sure-footed in the snow. (As Chevrolet's advertisements said, "How do you winterize a Corvair? You roll the windows up.") Corvairs had a fully unibody design, which offers incredible strength while providing significant weight savings over a traditional frame-on-body design.

The Corvair also had a four-wheel independent suspension, which enabled it to provide a level of ride comfort that was significantly better than what drivers got from other compact cars of the day. The efficiency of the unibody construction and the six-cylinder engine provided surprisingly good gas mileage. My father, who had a 1962 model, said that, depending on driving conditions, these cars could easily achieve gas mileage of over twenty-five miles per gallon.

In the first several years of the model, Chevrolet sold over two hundred thousand annually. The innovative design made it very versatile. It was offered in coupes, convertibles, sedans, wagons, minivans, and pickups. Chevy also made a turbocharged version with 180 horsepower. The turbo version was designed to help compete with the Ford Mustang.

Nader didn't give the Corvair credit for all of its innovations, but history has in part vindicated the Corvair. It has developed a loyal following, with numerous Corvair car clubs active today. Many of the state-of-the-art engineering features, such as the four-wheel independent suspension, the unibody construction, the versatile chassis, and the fuel-efficient design, are now common automotive offerings.

This wasn't the only time that the media took a prejudiced stance against American manufacturers. While it is true, they had ammunition against the Big Three in the 1970s and early 1980s, but by the 1990s, the quality gap had narrowed significantly. By 2008, GM had fewer National Highway Traffic Safety Administration (NHTSA) complaints than Toyota (Rattner). And yet I cannot count the number of articles criticizing GM vehicles. I have read articles that described vehicles made by a foreign competitor with words like "Spartan, "firm," and "quirky," whereas a domestic vehicle with similar characteristics would be described as "cheap," "rough," or "ugly." A slight change in the verbiage from one review to the other can create a strong impression.

Retired GM vice chairman Bob Lutz cited the hostile media as one of many factors that harmed GM. He compared consumer reviews that rated the Chevrolet Prizm and Chrysler's Eagle Talon. These cars had identical engineering and were made by the same workers as their Japanese sister cars, but they were rated lower than the Japanese versions. His theory was that even consumers didn't want to besmirch the reputation of the Japanese brands, but they would badmouth the American brands. He felt that the media created a culture in which American products were viewed as inferior. He described the American media's treatment of GM as "increasingly hostile...[it] loved picking on the big, dumb guy" (Lutz, 2011).

The *Wall Street Journal* reported that according to a 1980 Harbour and Associates report, the average GM car had 7.4 defects, while the average Japanese car had 2.0. But by 1993, J.D. Power and Associates reported the average GM car had 1.08 defects and the average Japanese car had .84 (as cited in Thompson and Strickland). In 2005, the Chevrolet Impala beat the Toyota Camry in initial quality. The Chevrolet Impala was also a *Consumer Reports* recommended buy. The gap had virtually disappeared, but the prejudice remained. Many reports continued to portray GM and other US manufacturers as substandard and the choice of the uninformed. Chevrolet's marketing manager, Jim Campbell, in response to the Impala's quality awards, was quoted as saying, "You don't change perceptions overnight" (Mateja).

Another point on which to critique the media is their portrayal of GM vehicles' fuel-economy performance. By 2008, when gasoline prices had skyrocketed to over $4 per gallon, the mainstream media had convinced the American public that they had to buy smaller foreign cars in order to realize higher fuel economy. Toyota seemed to be the chosen manufacturer, and it seemed totally incapable of error. The facts, however, tell a different story. In 2005, the combined fuel rating (average of city miles per gallon and highway miles per gallon) for a midsize Toyota Camry with a 3-liter V6 engine was 21 miles per gallon, whereas the 2005 full-sized Chevrolet Impala with a 3.4-liter V6 engine got a combined 22 miles per gallon.

Perhaps the most blatantly biased of all portrayals of GM products was the flagrant NBC video footage of the side-saddle gas tanks on the 1973–1987 pickup trucks. NBC showed footage of a car striking the side of one of these pickups and the pickup exploding into a ball of fire. NBC faked the shot by creating a small-explosive charge fire just before the impact, thus guaranteeing an explosion. Had GM perpetrated a comparable lie, it never would have lived it down, but as the media had executed it, all GM got for the airing of the fraudulent footage was an apology. A major news network falsified and distorted a report, but it didn't seem to harm its reputation, because the media were still able to portray GM as the villain.

The media would frequently describe the problems facing GM and other domestic manufacturers into the early 2000s as being the result of competition from high-quality imports from Europe and Japan. While some of the imports did have higher quality than the domestics, many of them didn't. But all imports were lumped together, creating a distinct impression that all imports were good and all domestics were inferior. A few slight words one way or another can make or break a sales presentation or a product review.

The frequent portrayal of GM's products in an undesirable light, no matter how undeserving, magnified the burdens that the UAW and the US government placed on General Motors. Even GM's vice chairman, Bob Lutz, made a similar observation. It doesn't make sense for any media outlet to portray the products of one of the largest advertisers in the world in any other way but in a fair and accurate manner. Why so many in the media show favoritism for imports over domestic vehicles is unexplainable.

The Dealers

Alfred P. Sloan felt that the franchise system was "the best one for manufacturers, dealers, and consumers" (Sloan). It was under his leadership in 1929 that GM established Motors Holding Corporation, a division of General Motors that furnished capital to dealerships and helped them establish good business practices. The capital, in essence, made

Motors Holding a shareholder of the dealership until the dealer repaid the funds. Not all dealerships participated in this program; it was geared primarily for start-ups or dealership expansions. But it underscores Sloan's understanding of the need for a dealer body. Sloan realized that the complexity of the transactions involved in the purchase of a new automobile was best served by experts in local markets.

Automobile dealers make significant investments in facilities whose sole purpose is to sell and service automobiles. Dealers have to properly present the new cars, recondition the trade-ins, and provide quality service, all the while operating under the gaze of federal, state, and local governments. They must also strike a balance between satisfying the demands of the factory and those of the customers, while trying to earn a profit. Just like any other system, this model leaves room for unscrupulous individuals.

Just as one bad apple will spoil the barrel, a few bad dealers tarnish the reputation of the "quality dealers." Quality business practices in general have been under attack in recent years. The forgoing of traditional product messages for a short-term sales boost now dominates the entire industry. By focusing purely on price and eliminating the value of the vehicle, dealers and manufactures undermined themselves. The unqualified successes of this revised marketing philosophy eventually lead to the product being viewed negatively.

The success of dealers who employed marketing tactics bordering on trickery led to an escalating pricing game, putting consumers in the position of pitting one dealer against another. Rather than consumers waiting for the new models to arrive so that they would have the latest innovations in safety, economy, and style, they would simply wait for the next sale. The automobile business, especially with domestic brands, became all about gimmicks and little about the true value and quality of the product.

Dealerships started down a slippery slope when they began advertising new vehicles for one hundred dollars over invoice, then fifty, then a thousand below invoice, and finally two thousand below invoice on newly redesigned models. I've seen ads for domestic vehicles that offer ten thousand dollars off. My personal favorite is when these dealers sign up with a direct-mail company. They send mock checks to consumers that are good for up to two thousand dollars if they purchase a car during an exclusive three-day sale. I had a friend tell me that his son stepped into a dealership during one of these sales. The young man got real excited and said, "Dad! They're going to give me nineteen hundred dollars toward a new truck." His father, who had been in business for himself for many years, replied, "Do you really think that a perfect stranger is going to give you nineteen hundred dollars with no strings attached?"

These ads and marketing programs all sound great at face value, but when the domestic dealers, GM dealers included, advertise new vehicles in such a distressed manner and the foreign brands do not, that, in a de facto way, positions American products as inferior to those of their competitors.

These dealers started selling cars in numbers of which they had never dreamed, and perhaps some were erroneously convinced that they were gaining in the market against the foreign competitors. Certainly, the factory was convinced that these "movers and shakers," as the factory calls them, were doing just that. In fact, they were only making gains against the smaller dealers in more rural areas who were still marketing and selling automobiles based upon value, quality, and service. These small dealers knew full well that there was no way any dealer could sell a new car or truck for two thousand dollars below invoice and remain in business.

Rational, business-minded individuals know they cannot sell products below their cost. I'm reminded of the story of the two pencil salesmen. One salesman was selling his pencils for six cents apiece and the other for four cents each. The first salesman asked the second, "How can you sell those pencils for four cents? They cost you five cents." The second salesman said, "I make up for it in volume; I sell a lot of them." Naturally, the more he sold, the more he lost, just like any of these domestic dealers who employed similar tactics.

What these dealers discovered was that if they offered these distressed prices on new cars and trucks, many customers would not question anything beyond the price of the car. This left the door open for the dealers to have really aggressive finance and insurance (F&I) departments. Many dealers focused a large amount of their efforts there. An unusually large spread between what the bank charges the dealer and what the dealer charges the customer for interest is the first area of profit opportunity. While many dealers make it a policy to charge bank rates, others charge the customer as much as 3 percent more. An additional 3 percent added to the interest rate on a $20,000 loan amounts to an additional $1,500 if a customer chooses to take the full sixty months to pay the loan in full.

The F&I departments didn't stop there. They noticed that an increasing number of customers were trading in vehicles that had negative equity, so they urged these customers to purchase gap insurance. Negative equity is when a customer owes more on the car than its current value at the time of trade. Several factors contribute to negative equity. A simplified explanation is that the customer wants a certain car with a specific payment in mind, and often, in an effort to achieve that payment, the term or length of the contract is extended. During the first couple of years of a loan, the car depreciates faster than the payments on the car can be made, and if customers choose to trade in their car during this period, they likely have negative equity. Usually, if the customers wait one or two years, they will have positive equity and will be in a better position to trade. As we all know, necessity is the mother of invention, and insurance companies have developed gap insurance so that in the event the vehicle becomes a total loss in an accident, the insurance company pays the difference between what is owed and what the vehicle is worth. I have seen some F&I departments that charged over six hundred dollars for this coverage. Normally, it is sold for around three hundred dollars or less.

The F&I departments have a whole menu of products to offer customers after they've negotiated what they feel is the most important part of the transaction. Customers are given professional presentations on the value of having the regular scheduled oil changes figured into the cost of the loan. They also encourage customers to add extended warranties by scaring them with scenarios showing the costs of specific repairs.

Don't get me wrong: extended warranties, gap insurance, and some of the other products are quality products that, depending on circumstances, buyers should seriously consider. But in some instances, these products are offered at significantly inflated prices in an effort to cover the advertised discount of the car.

A few years ago, I overheard a conversation with an F&I representative from a large dealership who bragged about a deal that he had made that week for the benefit of someone who managed a small dealership. In a boisterous way, he said, "I grossed twenty-eight hundred dollars in F&I on one deal this week." Most of the listeners didn't pay attention to what he had said, but the manager of the small dealership knew what he was talking about, and he replied, "How do you sleep at night?" His answer: "Very well."

While these practices have been around for quite a while, recently enacted policies make them more prominent and problematic. These policies, combined with a less-than-stellar service experience, caused significant damage to GM's customer loyalty. When a service department's sole function is to generate revenue, the customer becomes simply a number. If a customer has a problem with his or her car and it gets corrected in a timely manner with a degree of concern from the service team, the customer will most likely develop a deep connection to the dealership and the products it represents. Customer loyalty cannot be purchased with a fancy ad or marketing campaign or fast-talking personnel. Rather, it must be earned, one customer at a time, one transaction at a time.

I've been told by people in the industry that a significant percentage of new-car dealers, especially dealers who sell domestic cars, lose money on new-car sales each year. Naturally, dealers must earn a profit, so other departments, which the industry refers to as the "back end," need to pick up the slack. I've discussed the importance of the F&I departments, and I've also mentioned the service departments' significance in terms of generating profits for some of these dealerships, but I haven't mentioned how some of the more unscrupulous service departments treated General Motors.

Some of these dealerships were unfair not only to customers but to GM. General Motors keeps track of warranty expenses and it knows, based upon the failure rates designed into cars and on statistical analyses of real-world results, what any given dealership should incur in warranty expenses. Some dealers think they are clever, and try to take advantage of corporate incompetence, but it always catches up with them.

According to GM employees, a certain dealership tried to take advantage of a known problem with brake rotors by replacing a significant volume of them under warranty. GM audited the dealership and literally had a dump-truckload of brake rotors to inspect. I know of one customer who brought his low-mileage Blazer to one of these dealers just a week after purchasing it from a reputable dealership. He had been on the interstate and noticed that a tire seemed to be slightly out of balance. The dealership replaced all four rotors. The salesman who sold him the truck and had driven it prior to selling it asked if the customer had heard a vibration when he braked. He said no, but the dealership replaced them anyway.

Alfred Sloan wrote that a high prevalence of bad merchandising practices began to surface around 1950. He discussed the increasing number of dealers "bootlegging cars." Bootlegging is a practice in which a new-car dealer sells a car to a used-car dealer for the latter to resell. The problem, as the factory views it, is that a customer who would otherwise have purchased the vehicle from a franchised dealership ends up purchasing it from a used-car dealer who cannot provide warranty support. It decreases the value of the product and reduces brand loyalty (Sloan). Bootlegging has the same result as when a new-car dealer in one country sells a car to a resident of another country (for example, when a US dealer sells to a Canadian customer). A vehicle sold this way is called a "gray market" car.

Sloan also wrote about "price packing," which is a practice in which a dealer bumps up the price of a new car in an effort to create a greater profit margin. The increased profit margin enables the dealer to show a greater allowance on the customer's trade. The practice of price packing diminished when the federal government required that the Monroney sticker be affixed to the side window of every new car sold in the United States. The Monroney label is the automobile industry's name for the vehicle's window sticker, which states what the car should be sold for. But some dealers circumvented this by simply putting a "bump" sticker alongside the Monroney label. When a customer asked one salesperson what the extra sticker was for, the salesperson replied, "Well, this one [the Monroney label] is what we paid for the car [not true], and this one is what we marked it up to."

Another practice that has harmed the industry is "lowballing." If customers simply fail to commit to all of the high-pressure tactics, the dealership will offer them a ridiculously low price to compare with prices at other dealerships. Competing dealers admit they can't beat it, and the customer eventually returns to the original dealership. When the customer then accepts the offer, the dealership sales manager comes in and says that the price was a mistake and that the dealership couldn't stay in business if it sold cars at that price. One former salesman told me that about 75 percent of these customers then go ahead and accept the higher price. He also said that the ads his former employer ran included all of the rebates on a given vehicle even though most people wouldn't qualify for them.

All automobile manufacturers have dealers who engage in poor merchandising, but because GM had the largest dealer network, and therefore the largest customer base, it stood to lose the most when customers were alienated by these practices. Unfortunately for GM, the industry seemed to glorify lower operational standards, and while this was happening, customer satisfaction and loyalty diminished, as did the brand's image. Portraying vehicles as distressed merchandise created an aura of inferiority around domestic autos and allowed the foreign brands to capture more market share. It also implemented other unprincipled actions, which further deteriorated GM's market share and image.

GMAC and the 2008 Financial Crash

In 2006, GM sold a 51 percent interest in its GMAC subsidiary for $14 billion. The sale provided much-needed cash to GM, which lost $10.6 billion in 2005, but it also lowered GM's share of GMAC's profits. From 2003 to 2006, GMAC contributed $2.8 billion per year to GM's profit. During the same period, GM's profit from its automotive operations lost an average of $1.8 billion per year (Healey). It was hoped that separating GMAC from GM would: 1. provide GM with sufficient cash or liquidity to finance the turnaround in its automotive operations that was under way, and 2. increase the rating or quality of GMAC's bonds and thus lower its cost of borrowing. The lower borrowing costs would enable GMAC to provide lower, more competitive interest rates to consumers.

GMAC, known for being one of the largest automotive lenders in America, also had a division called ResCap that provided home mortgages. When the housing bubble burst in 2008, ResCap's losses forced GMAC into a government bailout (GMAC's auto lending operations were profitable). The US government eventually provided GMAC, later renamed Ally, with $17.2 billion in bailout funds. Ally placed the ResCap mortgage unit into bankruptcy in 2012 (Bomey).

The bailout was necessary, because GMAC provided the vast majority of GM and Chrysler dealers with floorplan (revolving loans to dealers for the cars that dealers have in inventory), and it was one of the largest automotive lenders in the country. The loss of GMAC would have eliminated the ability of the majority of GM and Chrysler dealers from stocking cars. Without inventory, dealers could not sell cars and without sales, the government's efforts to rescue the automakers would have been in vein.

The financial crash of 2008 was driven in part by corporate greed, government mismanagement of the housing market, and consumers' willingness to purchase properties that in some cases they knew were not affordable. Several things happened that preceded the tragic collapse of the financial system.

Part of the problem is that some financial models reward short-term investing over innovation. The speculative-alternative financial instruments that contributed to the 2008 financial collapse highlight the dysfunctional nature of big finance. Financial experts created mathematical formulas that provided great returns for a few years, but one of the fundamental flaws was that prices of goods and services do not always go up. If house values always went up, then the financial crisis would not have occurred to the extent that it did. However, the prices of houses declined when the supply of houses exceeded demand and consumers' disposable income declined. House supply exceeded demand because of overbuilding, a symptom of easy credit. The decline in disposable income was a symptom of skyrocketing fuel and food prices.

The 2008 financial collapse was primarily the result of the plummeting value of the Mortgage-Backed Securities that the financial institutions had created. Simply stated, banks originated subprime (high-risk) loans; they then sold them to larger banks that, in turn, chopped the loans into pieces and bundled those pieces into a portfolio consisting of large numbers of small pieces of whole loans. These financial instruments are called Mortgage-Backed Securities (MBS). Investors purchased the MBS, because of the interest payments on the mortgages they contained. When the MBS got sold to even larger institutions, the repackaged portfolios became AAA-rated securities.

In November 2013, JP Morgan Chase reached a $13 billion settlement deal with the federal government for JP's role in misrepresenting the value of MBS to investors. The state of Maine brought suit against Standard & Poor's, one of the rating agencies that gave MBS AAA ratings, because, according to Maine's attorney general, Janet Mills, "S&P knew its analytical models could not adequately assess these complicated securities but...it continued to rate the products anyway" (Richardson, Whit). Former Federal Reserve chairman Alan Greenspan expressed concern over the complexity of these instruments and the process by which they were developed, and he had access to two hundred of the finest economic minds in the world. At some point in the process, some of the smaller institutions provided some loan guarantees, or Credit Default Swaps (CDS), on the value of the securities. When individual home owners started to default in large numbers, the value of the MBS became almost worthless. The companies that provided the CDS could not insure the losses.

The financial meltdown of 2008 also had its roots in government intervention with the financial process. In 1992, quasi-government banks Fannie Mae and Freddie Mac were an instrumental part of Congress's plan to increase home ownership. Fannie and Freddie were to increase funding for affordable housing (Wallison and Pinto). Then, in 1995, the Clinton administration's Community Reinvestment Act required banks to demonstrate that they were making loans to underserved communities. These loans had a higher risk and a lower quality than traditional loans (Wallison and Pinto). Daniel B. Jeffs, founder of the Direct Democracy Center, stated that the actions taken in 1992 required Fannie Mae to get its budget approved by Congress. The combined actions of 1992 and 1995 allowed the Chairman of the House Financial Services Committee, Barney Frank, and other allies to exert pressure on Fannie and Freddie to relax lending standards to increase home ownership (Jeffs).

Fannie and Freddie were set up by the government in part to lower the cost of homeownership by purchasing mortgages from smaller lenders, thereby freeing up money for more loans. As of 2010, Freddie and Fannie held over five trillion dollars in US residential debt and were responsible for up to 75 percent of new mortgages in 2009 (Francis). The St. Louis Federal Reserve analyzed Fannie and Freddie's role and confirmed that it purchased risky MBS, but claimed it wasn't the result of the affordable-housing mandate. A Moody's analysis stated that it was for seeking profits from higher loan yields (Khimm). The Securities and Exchange Commission sued former Fannie and Freddie executives for misleading investors by saying its exposure to MBS was in the billions when it was really tens of billions more than that (Hall). In the end, it was a combination of political intervention from Congress and the Clinton administration, combined with Fannie and Freddie's appetite for risky MBS, that enticed a large number of unscrupulous lenders to originate loans to high-risk consumers and cause the financial meltdown of 2008.

The MBS were built upon a hollow foundation. The houses were real, but the demand for houses was overinflated. Demand for houses was the result of easy credit that allowed individuals to purchase homes that they could not afford. Higher sales led to more supply or inventory from home builders. When mortgage defaults started to increase, the oversupply caused a sharp decline in home values.

When house values declined, the MBS became worthless and the enormous sums of money that banks invested were lost overnight. Because many financial institutions had too high a percentage of assets invested in these securities, they lacked the diversity to absorb the losses, and the American taxpayer was forced to bail out insolvent firms. The crisis was further exacerbated by a Financial Accounting Standards Board (FASB) accounting change that mandated that companies value assets on their books based upon the current market value. This rule is called "mark-to-market." The problem is that the MBS values plummeted and banks had to increase capital to account for the accounting write-downs on the MBS (Epstein). The rule was eventually changed, but not before it contributed to the financial crisis.

Large financial institutions can still get better returns on capital by purchasing other speculative financial instruments instead of loaning the money to small-business owners trying to expand their businesses. Since the financial crisis, numerous news reports have expressed concern over the loose monetary policy of the Federal Reserve, only to have small-business owners say that the banks are not lending money. Part of the reason for banks' not wanting to lend money is due to increased federal regulations and loan requirements, and the other part is because of alternative financial instruments. Without capital for businesses to invest, they cannot hire new people. This is an important factor in the nation's continued economic stagnation.

The complete financial freeze in 2008 and early 2009 eliminated the ability for GM and Chrysler to seek traditional financial methods to fund their operations. The resulting lack of liquidity forced the US government to either bail out the auto companies or watch an enormous portion of the nation's economy disappear overnight.

Chapter Five

Management Missteps

M
any of the major factors that contributed to the recent bankruptcy of General Motors were described by GM management to Congress as reasons for their lack of competitiveness. All of the Big Three domestic manufacturers had to deal with these problems. Ford, GM, and Chrysler all had similar union contracts and faced the same government regulations, media biases, and dealer problems. So how did Ford escape the same misfortune that befell GM and Chrysler? What separated GM and Chrysler from Ford?

When Bill Ford took over as chief executive officer of Ford Motor Company in 2006, he had to try to fix the gauntlet of problems left by the previous management. He recognized that Ford needed a different set of skills to complete the turnaround. He personally oversaw the search for a new CEO, looked for the best of the best, and chose a former executive vice president of Boeing, Alan Mulally. Mulally received a bachelor of science degree and master of science in aeronautical and astronautical engineering from the University of Kansas. He also received a master's degree in management as a Sloan fellow from MIT's Sloan School of Management (Ford Motor Company). Hiring him would prove to be a brilliant move. (And it is rather ironic: the man who played a key role in saving Ford earned a master's degree in a business discipline not only from Alfred P. Sloan's alma mater but also from a school of business that bears his name.)

Ford came close to filing for bankruptcy several years before GM and Chrysler were forced into it after the 2008 financial crisis. Articles written about Ford at the time said that Ford was out of money, out of product, and out of time. But because banks were willing to lend money in 2006, Ford managed to escape bankruptcy. When Alan Mulally became chairman of Ford in 2006, he secured billions in capital, while the banks were lending, in order to fund Ford's resurgence.

After studying the actions of GM's and Chrysler's management, President Obama's head of the Presidential Task Force on the Auto Industry, Stephen Rattner, was quoted in an October 26, 2009, *Automotive News* article as saying that the task force found "stunningly poor management." In the same article, Rattner described GM as having "perhaps the weakest finance operation any of us had ever seen in a major company." Of GM's CEO, Rick Wagoner, he said he was "likable, dedicated, and generally knowledgeable" but that he "set a tone of 'friendly arrogance' that seemed to permeate the organization." Rattner also found that GM had initially made little contingency planning, because Wagoner refused to consider bankruptcy (Rattner). Given the unpopular label "Government Motors," Wagoner, while not always correct, was not always wrong. Regardless of the task force's findings, when the government fired Wagoner, it set a dangerous precedent of government control over free enterprise.

Make no mistake about it, there were significant stressors acting against General Motors for decades, and these stressors deserve much of the blame. But decades of GM management have to share a portion of the responsibility for the company's problems. Directions were chosen and decisions were made that placed the company in a precarious position in late 2008. The GM bankruptcy, in terms of assets, was the fourth largest in US history.

Any bankruptcy proceeding has significant levels of complexity, but a bankruptcy of GM's magnitude simply boggles the mind. It was accomplished from start to finish in forty days. Critics contend that some groups got a much better deal than others. The bondholders, who traditionally are first in line for payment, got pennies on the dollar. They were offered a mere 10 percent of the new company, with the option to buy another 5 percent. The government said that because over 50 percent of the bondholders accepted the offer, that was enough to force the remainder of the stakeholders to take it. (Just a point to ponder: a significant percentage of the outstanding bonds were held by large institutions. What percentage of these institutional investors were being strong-armed by the government because they were operating with federal bailout funds? Unfortunately, no one knows.)

Under the original proposal, the current stockholders of the "old GM" were supposed to get a token 1 percent of the new company, but the plan changed at some point and the stockholders got nothing. Some of these people had held GM stock for years, through good times and bad, and in some cases this stock represented their life's savings.

The unions ended up with 17 percent of the company, which was shifted to the Voluntary Employee Beneficiary Association (VEBA) trust, which manages their health-care fund. As generous as this sounds, it represents billions of lost dollars. The unions also had to finally forgo the practice of job banks and had to make wage and other benefit concessions. GM's salaried retirees had lost their insurance in 2008, prior to the bankruptcy. Current salaried employees also had to take pay and benefit cuts. Numerous communities all over the country have also suffered, as GM has laid off thousands of salaried and union workers and shuttered a dozen plants.

One of the reasons Congress allowed the bailout of the automakers was to prevent key suppliers from suffering the same fate. Suppliers play a major role in the entire industry. Other automotive manufacturers were concerned that without essential components from some of these suppliers, they would also be forced to cease operations until suitable substitutes could be procured. The economy would have been devastated if multiple manufacturers had shuttered their plants because several of their suppliers had gone bankrupt, resulting in shortages of parts.

There were almost 1,400 dealers who were targeted for closure as a result of the government-sanctioned bankruptcy. Remember, GM had originally proposed to reduce the number of dealerships to 4,700 by 2012 and to 4,100 by 2014, but the automotive advisory task force rejected the proposal and forced GM to make deeper and quicker reductions.

The original plan was to focus primarily on metropolitan and suburban markets, where dealer overcrowding was most evident. The revised plan sacrificed an additional five hundred dealers in rural markets where they, according to the congressional hearings, enjoy a full 10 percent market-share advantage as compared with the metropolitan markets. The cuts were sped up to become effective by October 2010, with virtually no financial remuneration. The cuts were reportedly some of the most painful tasks that some of the executives had ever implemented.

The American taxpayer was generous in supporting the automotive bailouts. Not only has the US government, as the 363 acquirer, pledged tens of billions of dollars in funding during the bankruptcy, it also provided approximately eighteen billion dollars before the bankruptcy, which the government said it was unlikely to recover. (The phrase "363 acquirer" refers to section 363 of the US bankruptcy code. The acquirer purchases the bankrupt assets, which are made free and clear of claims via a court order.) This pre-bankruptcy funding was meant to enable GM to organize the bankruptcy. Taxpayers provided over fifty billion dollars in funding to GM.

The government recouped approximately twenty-three billion dollars from GM's repayment of the loans and from the sale of GM stock (Rosevear). The remaining shares needed to be sold for an estimated fifty-three dollars per share for the US Treasury to break even on the funding (Lawder). In December 2013, the federal government sold its remaining shares in GM. The estimated cost to taxpayers was $10.5 billion. The Center for Automotive Research claimed: that for every dollar the federal government spent, on the automotive bailout, it actually saved taxpayers eight dollars, because thousands of jobs were saved (Nelson). When unemployment goes up, government loses income from taxes and it spends more money due to increased unemployment payments.

Under the terms of the bankruptcy, the government became a majority shareholder in exchange for billions of dollars' worth of funding, but the government still held about seven billion dollars' worth of GM debt and 61 percent of the company's equity. The other owners were the UAW's health-care trust, which got 17.5 percent, the Canadian government, which got 11 percent, and the bondholders, who got 9.8 percent of the new GM (*Huffington Post*/Associated Press). GM's CEO, Ed Whitacre, was pleased to announce that GM had paid the seven-billion-dollar loan early, since he didn't like GM's being referred to as "Government Motors." Ironically, he unexpectedly left shortly after uttering those remarks. Whitacre said that the board was aware of his plan to be a short-term CEO the day he took the job. But the timing raises the question: Was the Obama administration upset about Whitacre's comments, and did it pressure him to leave before the initial public offering (IPO) of the new GM stock? While unfortunate, Whitacre's departure was designed to provide stability for the corporation after the IPO, because he felt that a departure soon after the IPO would undermine the value of the stock. The IPO yielded for the government over eleven billion dollars of the fifty billion it had invested, and GM has since announced increased sales and its first profits since 2006 (Isidore).

Cubical Justification

A long-standing criticism of General Motors has been its bureaucratic culture. In 2013, a GM executive said that by reducing or eliminating bureaucracy, the company can add those saved dollars to product development or to its bottom line (Colias, GM Taps Manufacturing ...). In fairness to GM, most large organizations suffer from some degree of bureaucracy. Retired GM vice chairman Robert Lutz wrote that despite mediocre results, many large organizations follow "the process" (bureaucracy) because it is predictable. He went on by commenting that GM was known as a "great destroyer of capital," because of its self-perpetuating bureaucracy that cost more but produced less. Lutz also gave former GM CEOs Jack Smith and Rick Wagoner credit for recognizing the bureaucracy as being unsustainable. Smith and Wagoner made significant improvements in GM's bureaucratic structure, but the turnaround efforts fell short when the 2008 financial crisis occurred (Lutz, 2013).

Bureaucracy's root cause can be found in "cubical justification." A former regional vice president of a now-defunct major retail chain store explained this principle and cited it as the cause of the demise of many of America's once-great businesses. Cubical justification is the process wherein a large corporation or a government places newly-educated individuals (usually people with an MBA) into relatively high-level positions within the organization. These people often have less real experience than their subordinates and are not always aware of how the various parts of the company integrate with each other. Therefore, inexperienced MBAs seem to constantly tweak and create policies, procedures, and informational requirements in order to justify their job.

The same can be said of federal and state governments. New politicians in a legislature create the same phenomenon. The constant and often unnecessary changes and requirements cause everyone downstream of the "new rules" to spend significant amounts of time and resources maintaining "compliance" rather than focusing on the real needs of the customer/citizen.

The net result of cubical justification is bureaucracy. Bureaucracy almost always distracts subordinates and firms from their given or productive tasks in favor of performing nonproductive and unnecessary actions. The more the phenomenon occurs, the greater the chances that the company or government will suffer.

All large organizations, including the government, are susceptible to cubical justification, because of their complex organizational structures. The importance of a good education like an MBA is therefore necessary in corporate America. However, the MBA requirement has created another glass ceiling, but this time it doesn't deal with gender. Some of the greatest American entrepreneurs of the last century built enormous industrial companies and fortunes without an MBA. They started with a small firm and a lot of ambition. They knew how the several parts of the company fit and built upon each other. The more removed some of these great corporations got from that "understanding," the more likely the companies were to fail. I am not saying companies should eliminate MBAs, but I am saying that just because someone doesn't have one, that shouldn't prevent him or her from being elevated to executive positions.

I am reminded of a story. Several years ago, a GNP executive was giving some people a tour of one of the mills. The executive and his guests passed by a seasoned paper-machine tender. He was sitting in a chair and appeared not to be doing anything. One of the people commented on that fact, to which the senior executive was rumored to have said, "When I see him sitting there like that, it means his machine is running good and he is making me money." What some inexperienced management personnel and most politicians don't understand is that sometimes less is more.

Leaders and Finance Syndrome

Management's failure wasn't the result of a revolution but rather was sealed by evolution. Responsibility cannot lie solely with the management team in place at the time of the bankruptcy, because some of the company's problems were from management errors that were decades old.

It would be easy to point to Alfred P. Sloan's retirement as the beginning of the end, but that wouldn't be fair to the dedicated staff that he left behind. Upon Sloan's retirement as chairman of the board at the age of eighty, in 1956, GM had an experienced, well-trained staff with some of the finest minds at the helm. Changes to GM were slow and some may seem insignificant, but the long-term ramifications created an irrefutable trajectory that cannot be disputed.

According to an article in *Automotive News*, GM's CEO, Harlow Curtice, shifted power away from GM's New York office to its Detroit headquarters. This shift evidently involved other significant changes, because Sloan felt that the company should not abandon the financial systems and controls that he, Donaldson Brown, and Albert Bradley established in the 1920s (Wright). Brown was a former treasurer of DuPont Company before becoming vice president of finance at GM (Virginia Tech). Bradley was elected to the GM finance committee in 1933 and succeeded Sloan as chairman of the board in 1956 (General Motors). Curtice had a brilliant career at GM. In 1955, as CEO, he oversaw GM's transformation into the first corporation to earn over one billion dollars in a single year. He had a résumé of success and therefore won the argument. Sloan retired on April 2, 1956 (Wright).

The shift from New York to Detroit didn't result in a 180-degree reversal of the Sloan policies. It only marked the beginning of a slow divergence from them. As time went on, the corporation's separation from the Sloan policies became more and more pronounced. The change didn't become evident to the public, but a quick look at GM's post-Sloan management shows the increasing divergence, and the results prove the point.

People should remember that Sloan had graduated from MIT with a bachelor's degree in electrical engineering and came to GM via Durant's purchase of Hyatt Roller Bearing Company, of which Sloan was president (Pelfrey). Durant rolled Hyatt into a new company called United Motors in 1916 and made Sloan president. In 1918, this company was merged into General Motors, and Sloan became a vice president of GM and a member of its executive committee.

A list of GM chairmen since Sloan shows that only two of them—James M. Roche, who headed Cadillac, and Robert C. Stempel, who headed Chevrolet—had held a position as the head of a division. It is also worth mentioning that with the exception of Stempel and John G. Smale, all of the chairmen were either finance specialists, accountants, statisticians, or the like (General Motors). Stempel was an engineer and Smale was an outside director who led the ouster of Stempel in 1992.

The list of CEOs since Sloan reveals equally interesting facts. Charles E. Wilson, who was CEO from 1946 to 1953, was an engineer. Harlow H. Curtice followed him from 1953–1958. He had headed ACDelco and worked his way through the corporation from the humble beginnings of a bookkeeper (General Motors). With the exception of Roche and Stempel, the next nine GM CEOs were all accountants or finance specialists.

Given the dollar amounts involved in operating such a large corporation and the nature of the organization regarding labor relations, stockholder relations, and financing in general, it becomes apparent that a financial background is very important and perhaps necessary for the success of any company in tough economic times like these. But since GM's primary purpose is or was the manufacturing of automobiles, trucks, buses, locomotives, appliances, and subassemblies, an executive with a primary background in engineering or manufacturing is of equal or greater importance and benefit to the corporation, because too much financial control can be as bad or worse than not enough financial control. GM's severe financial problems in the early 1900s show the perils of too little financial control, and the events leading up to the bankruptcy show the ills of too much financial leadership.

The shift toward financial leadership had a delayed effect, because there were several powerful engineers who held prominent positions within the corporation. When men like Ed Cole, the father of the small-block Chevy, and Elliot "Pete" Estes, another terrific engineer who eventually became president of GM, retired, the focus on finance became more and more prominent. Any engineer with whom I have ever spoken had a firm grasp of how machinery worked and usually focused on how to make something better, stronger, or more durable. Many financially-minded people have as their natural tendency a focus on how to trim costs or make something cheaper. Making a process more cost-effective is a good thing, but when the drive to do so becomes obsessive, which it often does, it is reflected in the appeal of the product.

The difference between an engineering approach to solving a problem and the finance approach is what I term finance syndrome. Rather than invest the necessary funds to attack a product's shortcomings by addressing the root of the problem, some people try to find a marketing-based solution. An example would be a rebate, which in essence lowers the price to the point where a customer will accept shortcomings. If rebates are continually employed to make a product more appealing, it undermines the long-term value of the product in the eyes of the consumer.

Here is an example of how the two management styles view a problem. In 1953, General Motors introduced the Corvette to the world. The sporty design was more like a sculpture than a car. The 1953 Corvette didn't sell as expected, and the 1954 sales were even more disappointing. The pre-bankruptcy, financial-specialist generation of GM management would have devised a brilliant marketing scheme that, as its main focus, involved a once-in-a-lifetime incentive. Sales would have improved for the model year, and when sales declined again the next year, the company would have created an even more brilliant marketing plan. The process would have gone on for five or six years, after which GM would have canceled the car because there would not have been enough profitable demand for it.

As it happened, in the 1950s, GM's management was intrigued by a letter written by an engineer with a passion for racing. The letter to Chevrolet's chief engineer, Ed Cole, suggested some ideas to improve the model. Cole was so impressed that he decided to offer the man a position at Chevrolet. The man's name was Zora Arkus-Duntov, and he would become known as the "godfather of the Corvette."

In an interview with Arkus-Duntov, he recalled looking at the car and saying it "was a stylings car." But he couldn't figure out why the company chose the Chevrolet Blue Flame 6 as its engine. He successfully pushed Cole and Chevrolet to speed the development of the V8 engine program, which enabled GM to match the performance with the styling. The Corvette quickly became America's sports car and has remained an American icon of excellence.

There have been several instances in recent years in which a product was eliminated because GM management failed to address underlying issues with a particular model and chose instead to market it by offering incentives to customers. The Pontiac Motor Division is a good example. Observers can easily see the negative long-term results of the financial approach as compared with the engineering approach. It isn't necessary to list all of the Pontiacs that could have been improved, but a few like the Grand Prix, G6 and Torrent, thanks to shared platforms, may have allowed Pontiac to continue to "Build Excitement."

Product

As GM's management became more and more focused on finance, design began to take a back seat. In his memoir *Car Guys vs. Bean Counters: The Battle for the Soul of American Business*, Bob Lutz explained a brief history of GM design arrogance and the ensuing resentment that it generated among some in GM's management. Efforts were made to refocus product development away from GM's design department and to the product-planning department. Lutz characterized the product-planning department as "a department composed of recycled finance types."

Lutz said that product planners would determine market segments that warranted GM's presence, and then they would plan the car's interior and exterior size to the millimeter. Engineering and manufacturing would weigh in on what went where and how it was to be manufactured in an effort to maximize savings. Then design would be allowed to, in essence, connect the dots (Lutz, 2011). The new system led to increasingly boring look-alike designs. When the offerings from GM's major divisions all looked alike, consumers began slowly to seek other automakers' products.

GM made the exodus easier when it left the designs of key products virtually unchanged for years. With the emotional aspects removed from product development, the emotions were removed from the product, and consumers, therefore, didn't have compelling emotional reasons to purchase. As an outlet, some consumers sought imported cars, having been infected by the emotions of a flattering press that was enamored of foreign vehicles.

To his credit, GM's CEO, Rick Wagoner, was aware of the design dilemma, and he hired Lutz to be vice chairman of design in 2001. GM had made several revisions to its design system over the years, but it had failed to achieve the glory of the designs of the 1950s and 1960s. Lutz found a system that was rich with research and tried to quantify design. The system GM was using for vehicle development was one that relied on vehicle-line executives. Vehicle-line executives (VLEs) were in charge of vehicle development, and they were in essence program managers for individual vehicle programs.

The performance of VLEs was measured by stringent cost targets, timelines, assembly hours per vehicle, and the percentage of parts re-used from the previous vehicle. They were talented people, but the major flaw of the system was that they were also given responsibility for design. VLEs had the final say in the aesthetic judgment of interior and exterior components. Lutz said that most companies are lucky if they have two or three people capable of making such decisions. GM's system had fourteen VLEs. Lutz said no car company in the world had fourteen senior people capable of making such aesthetic judgments. The system was geared toward speed and costs. Designs that didn't appeal to consumer product clinics were often pushed through in order to meet the timing and budget (Lutz, 2011).

The result of GM's VLE system was an assortment of competent and reliable vehicles that lacked the aesthetic balance that catches the eye of the consumer and causes a "got to have" or "buy me" reaction. The style of the car is often the reason a consumer stops to look at it. When that was absent, the factory was forced to pay consumers to buy the cars by using rebates or low interest rates. Vehicles not only missed sales targets, but profit margins were reduced because of high incentive levels.

A vehicle that suffered from this type of "finance syndrome" was the Pontiac Aztek. This was GM's first attempt at a crossover vehicle, but it was so ugly that people had to sneak up on it just to get in it. Even GM vice chairman Bob Lutz, when asked "Would you call this ugly?" replied, "There is no other way to describe it." (The Aztek was based on the Montana minivan chassis, which it shared with the Chevy Venture, but the Aztek was styled to resemble more of an SUV than a van.) The vehicle never came even close to meeting sales targets. An *Automotive News* article quoted a GM executive, Ron Zarella, as saying the poor sales resulted from the company getting "a little greedy on the price."

Knudsen's Pontiac of the 1950s and 1960s wouldn't have designed anything that ugly from the start, and even if it had, Pontiac would have quickly redrawn the roofline and changed the rear hatch. His Pontiac would have restyled the front grille and eliminated the geometric cladding on the sides. The cladding didn't do anything for the design except to reaffirm its ugliness. The chassis was great and the vehicle's versatility was equally as impressive. It would have been a distinctive crossover for Pontiac, and it would have offered a unique alternative to the Chevy Equinox rather than a virtual clone, like the Torrent, which eventually replaced the Aztek.

Another styling disappointment, according to Lutz, was the 2004 Pontiac Grand Prix (Lutz, 2011). It wasn't the albatross that the Aztek was, but it lacked the "got to have" emotion of the 1997 through 2003 Grand Prix. When GM introduced the 1997 Grand Prix, it was a great success. It was bold and unique, and it was all Pontiac. For the first few years of that body style, it commanded significantly higher prices than the Chevy Lumina, and it even held its value better than the newer Impala. GM finally chose to redesign it seven model years later and went with an "evolutionary" design. Customers expected something bolder. It was a great car, but it didn't have the emotional appeal to guarantee success.

Pontiac used to be the number three automotive division in the country. Its mission was to provide driving excitement at an affordable price. Pontiacs were targeted to young consumers, people looking for a little more style and excitement than what the average midsize car offered. Cars that are not perceived as exciting or that are packaged and priced just above what the intended buyers can afford require a rebate in order to sell. The rebate lowers the long-term trade-in value or residual value and diminishes the brand's value.

When faced with unpopular cars like the Aztek and the later-model Grand Prix, financial experts choose the path of least financial resistance. Rather than create a long-term solution to some problems, they choose what will look better next quarter or maybe next year. This is not unique to GM, as all modern corporations seem to engage in such behavior. But had GM chosen the option with the higher initial cost and fixed the problems rather than pay customers to accept them, the results would have been remarkable. GM's success with the 2008 Malibu and Chevrolet Cruze prove it.

Had GM fixed the problem with the Aztek and met sales objectives, it may have justified the continuation of the Montana and Venture minivans. Had it fixed the Grand Prix, it would have made a significant difference in overall Pontiac sales. The midsize segment is one of the largest vehicle segments in the country. With just two major high-volume sales successes in the crossover and midsize segments, Pontiac might have escaped the government's demand that the division be axed.

These are just a few examples that demonstrate the dangers of the short-term view of marketing that permeated pre-bankruptcy GM. Vice chairman Bob Lutz described the decision not to build hybrids earlier as a good decision on paper, but the end result caused GM to forfeit its leadership position in perceived technological advancements to Toyota (Lutz, 2011). In Lutz's mind, the change in customer perceptions cost the company more money than the initial losses on the hybrids. GM ended up using some vehicle chassis to the point at which it could not justify a business case for continuing them, and when that happened, GM simply gave up that segment to its competitors.

One brilliant marketing plan that eventually backfired occurred after the September 11, 2001, attacks. In the tragic aftermath, GM created the zero-percent marketing campaign and "kept America rolling." GM estimated that the Keep America Rolling incentive program added one million sales of cars and trucks in the United States by year's end (Kisiel). Keep America Rolling almost single-handedly kept customers in the showroom. Its effects were so positive that it was said to have played a role in minimizing the 2001 recession.

A short time after that, when the markets started to return to normal, some of the competitors lamented that they couldn't afford to match the size of incentives that GM offered.

GM executive Rick Wagoner's response, in essence, was "Tough." He said that the incentives worked and they were here to stay. But even basic marketing classes teach that perpetual sales do nothing more than create a short-term solution to a long-term problem; they eventually reach a point where they lose their effectiveness.

Proof that fixing a vehicle's shortcomings with rebates is not the best solution can be found with the all-new 2013 Chevrolet Malibu. The car was very well styled and had a long list of improvements from the previous model, but consumers and critics were quick to point out the front-end styling didn't differentiate it enough from other models, and rear-seat legroom appeared to be cramped. Pre-bankruptcy GM would have added incentives, which reduce resale and lease residual values, until a fix could be incorporated into a scheduled freshening in the car's third or fourth year. Post-bankruptcy GM promptly ordered fixes to the car. The new 2014 Malibu, with fixes, was on dealer lots by the end of 2013. GM North America president Mark Reuss, an engineer, was quoted in *Automotive News* as saying, "When we see decay happening, or something that didn't work as well as we'd have liked it to, we'll go fix it" (Colias, "GM's new product...").

Distractions and Delays

Some may say that GM didn't have enough resources to make the needed changes to the various cars because it had so many models and divisions. We are reminded of the money that GM spent on Saab from 1990 to 2000, when it acquired the Swedish carmaker. Lutz said, "Frankly, I would have steered clear of this charming loser, and I later advocated sale or wind-down every chance I got." The Saab acquisition didn't produce manufacturing synergies, and every attempt to expand the division failed (Lutz, 2011). GM also purchased a 20 percent interest in Fiat, with an option to buy the rest of the company. And GM eventually paid Fiat two billion dollars to get out of the deal. At his first meeting with the automotive task force, Fiat's CEO, Sergio Marchionne, bragged about taking GM to the cleaners on the deal (Rattner). GM walked away with little to show for the investment, and it spent billions to get it.

Though the shift of power from the engineering side to the finance side occurred over many years, the effects appeared to surface around the time of Thomas Murphy's tenure as chairman. In his retirement speech to some employees, Lutz criticized the GM executive, who said that GM was in the business of making money. Lutz asked, "Would you eat at a restaurant that had such an attitude?" The attitude certainly became obvious during Roger B. Smith's era. It was during Smith's tenure that the imports began making significant inroads into GM's market share. A major part of the explanation for this is the length of time that GM kept virtually unchanged models on the market. The following models that were designed or introduced near the end of Murphy's career were still in production near the end of Smith's career.

POPULAR MODELS LIFE CYLE

Model	Year Introduced	Year Redesigned
Chevrolet Caprice	1977	1991
Chevrolet Celebrity	1982	1990 (Replaced)
Chevrolet Cavalier	1982	1995
Chevrolet Camaro	1982	1993
Chevrolet S10	1982	1994
Chevrolet C/K Pickup	1973	1988

These models represented not only a significant portion of Chevrolet's sales but a significant portion of other GM divisions' sales, because they used the same chassis. With only minor styling and engineering changes from the time the models were introduced to the final versions a decade later, customers lost interest in the brands and turned to GM's competitors.

During the Smith decade, GM did invest, but much of the investments were in other areas. During the 1980s, GM invested over seventy billion dollars to upgrade its plants. Much of the cost of the upgrades involved a significant increase in the number of robots used in the manufacturing process. The robots were installed in an effort to reduce GM's dependency on union labor in the manufacturing process (Thompson and Strickland).

In theory, automating plants was a brilliant idea, but the inflexibility that robots brought to the manufacturing process reduced the versatility of the plants (not to mention the famous stories of the robots painting each other and the embarrassment that ensued). The intent was to invest capital up front to lower future labor costs. The cost of labor to manufacture a car did go down. However, indirect labor costs went up, because there was significant growth in the need for highly skilled maintenance and repair crews (Lutz, 2011). Furthermore, the huge upfront capital expenditure appeared to delay product revisions. When GM, under Roger Smith's watchful eye, developed the GM 10 project in the 1980s (later known as GM's "W bodies": Grand Prix, Lumina, Regal, and Cutlass Supreme), it employed extensive levels of robotics in the manufacturing process, and as a result, it had one plant that could assemble only Grand Prix coupes.

Smith also oversaw a major reorganization of General Motors. He reduced divisional autonomy and redundancy in an effort to streamline the corporation. He created separate groups that were to be in charge of producing cars for the divisions. This apparently had the opposite effect, though, as critics have charged that it created more layers of bureaucracy and added additional layers of staff, which duplicated divisional staffs (Seaman, "Roger Smith's grand..."). The cookie-cutter styling and long design times I described earlier were apparently the result of this reorganization. This system was in place for a decade before all the divisions were finally rolled into one organization in the mid-1990s.

In an effort to diversify the company, Smith also oversaw the acquisition of Electronic Data Systems (EDS) and Hughes Aircraft Company. The amount of money spent on those acquisitions was reportedly over four billion dollars. While those investments were sold at a significant profit (ten times) about twenty years later, GM's market share slipped from 44.5 percent to 35.1 percent (Henry). (Americans should remember from the 1992 presidential election that, as a result of the EDS acquisition, Ross Perot became a member of the GM board for a short time. Perot, being a man of action, couldn't stand the levels of bureaucracy and the tendency to overanalyze that characterized GM's management.)

Roger Smith also oversaw tremendous investments of time and money in creating Saturn while the other divisions were starved of product. Numerous critics, including Robert Lutz, said that Saturn never made a profit and consumed over ten billion dollars in capital (Lutz, 2011). Another of Smith's investments was the automation of the plants. The amount of money that GM spent on robots in the 1980s was enough to buy Toyota outright. Here again, product suffered.

There appears to be no doubt that Roger Smith facilitated an environment in which GM's management was constantly creating another distraction in an effort to ignore the problems at hand. Another division, more robots, more subsidiaries, and corporate reorganization didn't address the problem of eroding market share and declining profit margins on automotive operations.

The cars that GM produced in the 1980s were fine automobiles. They were not perfect, but neither were anyone else's. Many of the changes made to the GM cars in the 1980s improved quality, reliability, and durability. GM continued to lose market share to the imports that were perceived to have much higher quality, although this perception was not always consistent with reality. As an example, Toyota pickups were gaining a reputation as very durable vehicles, but the trucks were notorious for severe rusting.

When Roger Smith retired in 1990, Robert Stempel assumed the reins. Stempel was the first engineer to head General Motors since Charles E. Wilson retired in 1953—and he was the last engineer that was promoted from within to head the corporation. Stempel had a long career at GM.

Despite his many years of success at GM, Stempel became the Herbert Hoover of the automobile industry. Shortly after he was named CEO, the country entered a long recession, slowing the nation's economic engine. Unfortunately, GM's cash flow was significantly harmed by the recession, and much-needed product development was slowed in an effort to conserve cash. And GM's market share had gone from about 45 percent in the mid-1970s to about 35 percent in the early 1990s. At one point in the early 1990s, GM was near bankruptcy and Stempel asked other GM executives to pray for the company (Chevrolet Motor Division).

The company was a financial wreck, and efforts to turn it around were not going as quickly as the board wanted. So Stempel, perhaps the most qualified person to head the company in decades, became the fall guy. John Smale, the former head of Proctor & Gamble, became the new chairman, and John Smith became the new CEO. These two accelerated the financial changes, and the company once again returned to profitability.

Brand Management

The 1990s reforms streamlined some of the bureaucracy that had piled up in the eighties under Roger Smith. GM shortened design times for new models and improved manufacturing efficiencies. It still seemed, however, that GM felt there was a financially-based solution to every problem. It hired Ron Zarella as a so-called "marketing czar." It was an effort to try to reproduce the style of brand management that Proctor & Gamble had success with.

The basic concept in brand management is that a marketing manager is put in charge of a particular product or brand. The manager and his or her team do extensive marketing research to redesign packaging, product content, and advertisements. Then they instruct the appropriate departments to fulfill the requests and to do a test run. GM's vice chairman Robert Lutz said that the problem with applying this concept to an automobile is that product changes cost hundreds of millions of dollars, and where a poorly performing toothpaste may linger for mere months, failed car models stay around for years (Lutz, 2011).

But GM executives were so convinced of the magic behind Zarella and his brand of management that, despite failures and plunging market share, he kept getting promoted. Remember, it was Zarella who said the reason the Pontiac Aztek failed was that GM got a little greedy on price. His ability to market automobiles was apparently overrated, as customers' perceptions of GM's products didn't improve.

GM's advertisements seldom focused on the quality of the cars or their features. The ads have for a long time focused on the deal of the month rather than the value of the product. The distressed environment that GM created with its ads, coupled with policies that encouraged dealers to do the same, created a perception that its products were indeed inferior. The message portrayed in the ads discredited the brand image that GM was trying to build. GM vice chairman Robert Lutz, who has been a longtime critic of GM ads, said they were good at talking about the sizzle of the steak but didn't talk about the steak itself. After the GM bankruptcy, Lutz was put in charge of advertising, and he made a shift in marketing policy when he announced "that the company was going to start talking about the 'steak' and not just the 'sizzle'" (Flint).

GM's system made each model a unique brand. This means that advertising dollars were divided up among GM's ninety brands. It resulted in so little expenditure per car line that the brands fell below consumer-awareness levels. Most of the new brand managers—as well as Ron Zarella—came from other industries and had little to no experience in how the automobile industry worked (Lutz, 2011).

Lutz said in order to develop some consistency in products, "a 'check the box' set of visual requirements was ultimately established for each make." Lutz went on to say that rather than focus on design excellence, GM brand managers were directing the design department to focus on "brand characteristics" (Lutz, 2011). The cars had all the brand characteristics, but they lacked the style and emotional factors that would motivate people to purchase them. The quality and reliability of the cars were on par with the competitors' cars, but the design of many of the models failed to create the enthusiasm that GM's trucks had.

Trucks escaped the malaise of the car program because the truck people were focused on building a better truck than GM's competitors, and the result was a string of successful products. The success of the truck programs caused GM, Ford, and Chrysler to all became too dependent on the profitable trucks. The problem with relying on trucks arose when gas prices soared in 2007 to 2008; truck and SUV sales plummeted. When sales plummeted, the car program was not strong enough to make up the difference.

GM and the Dealers

Zarella's continued promotions seemed to defy logic, as he not only failed to produce lasting improvements in market share but had a habit of annoying the company's dealers. Industry publications reported that he even said, at a dealers' meeting, that his obligation was to the shareholders and not to the dealers. He later apologized, but his candid remarks were only a verbal admission of what many dealers had felt for years.

Associated Press writer Ken Thomas wrote an article reporting some comments made by Steven Rattner, the former head of President Obama's automotive task force. Rattner described GM's board of directors as "utterly docile." Rattner went on to say, "Certainly, Rick and his team seemed to believe that virtually all of their problems could be laid at the feet of some combination of the financial crisis, oil prices, the yen-dollar exchange rate, and the UAW" (Thomas). GM's management blamed not only the aforementioned reasons for GM's maladies but also dealers and suppliers. GM has long ranked well below the industry average in dealer and supplier satisfaction.

One example of how GM used to work with dealers involves warranty policy and procedures. Previous to the last twenty-five years, GM was very strict in interpreting warranty repairs. If the needed repair was beyond limits or there was a question of abuse, the factory wouldn't pay. In an era when the domestic manufacturers had little foreign competition, the factory service staff was not always as knowledgeable or customer-oriented as it should have been.

Service representatives used to make regular rounds to dealerships every three weeks or so, and they instructed the dealers to have the cars with reported problems on site so that they could inspect them. They also gave the dealers strict instructions that they didn't want to speak with the customers.

One dealer reported, "Every time a factory representative walked through my door, he or she cost me a customer." He said that when Chevrolet was having camshaft problems with the 305 V8 engines, he had one disassembled for the service representative to inspect. The dealer directed the factory service representative to the workbench where the engine parts were and said, "Here's the problem with this car." The representative looked at it and said, "Hmm, that is nice. What am I looking at?" The dealer told her that she was looking at a camshaft from a 305, and she replied, "What is wrong with it?" The dealer pointed to the one round lobe on the shaft and said that it wasn't supposed to be round. She replied, "Oh, I see. I'm not buying it." The customer knew Chevrolet had a problem with the 305 and that Chevrolet wasn't willing to resolve it. The customer's next new car was not a Chevrolet.

By the late 1980s, GM had made a complete reversal on customer service. Management instructed staff to work with dealers and customers to increase customer satisfaction. In recent years, GM and its dealers have stepped up and supported its products with warranties and policies that exceed all reasonable customer expectations. The factory learned what many dealers had known for decades: happy customers become repeat customers.

Even with happy customers, manufacturers' policies can cause a dealer to lose sales to a competitor. Dealers often complain about a shortage of a key product or a glut of a slow-selling product. The industry term is "allocation." Dealers seldom have a problem getting hard-to-sell vehicles, but well-selling vehicles are sometimes impossible to get. Dealers in one part of the country may be overloaded with a specific product while others in other parts of the country are starved. It is a constant complaint among dealers. During the latter part of the 1990s, GMC apparently targeted specific regions for sales growth. It took GMC allocation from dealers in one region and gave it to dealers in others, creating a de facto double allocation. This meant that if a dealer sold one GMC, he or she could earn two. Chevrolet dealers in the targeted regions at the time were having a hard time replacing trucks that they had sold.

One of the largest Chevrolet dealers in Maine at the time would only have two dozen Silverados, while at the same time the GMC dealer across town had a couple of hundred Sierras. In a market with growing truck sales, this made it difficult for some dealers to compete effectively.

The ability to compete on a level playing field is a source of debate between dealers. Some dealers feel that incentive and recognition programs are structured to favor large dealers over smaller dealers. General Motors in recent years has had something called the Mark of Excellence program. There are two parts to this program. One part is designed to encourage dealership staff to improve their knowledge and performance. The other part of the program, Standards for Excellence, is designed to increase dealership performance.

Dealers tell me that in 2007, a Chevrolet dealer, regardless of size or market area, had to spend thirty-five thousand dollars to sign up, at which point he or she would be given a customer-satisfaction objective and a sales objective. If the dealer made the goal for the quarter, he or she would be given a pay bonus. The cost to sign up was the same for small dealers and large dealerships, and the way the bonus system worked made it difficult for small dealerships to recoup the sign-up cost.

The National Automotive Dealers Association (NADA) complained that the program offered larger dealers a greater return on investment than a smaller dealer could obtain. The program also encouraged larger dealers to cheapen the brand by advertising in a distressed manner in order to achieve sales goals. GM responded by modifying the program to enable a better return for smaller dealers, but numerous small dealers said that the program still favored the large dealers.

Many smaller dealers would prefer that the factory eliminate such recognition and incentive programs. Small dealers feel that eliminating the programs would place them on a level playing field with larger dealers by compelling everyone to refocus on the value of quality service to the consumer. During the bankruptcy hearings, GM testified that because there were too many dealerships, GM had to create these incentive programs to keep dealers profitable. GM cited the incentive programs as a partial justification for eliminating dealers.

Finally, during the last several years, GM has, at times, created policies that have in a de facto way forced dealers to sell cars at fixed prices. An example would be GM's Employee Price for Everyone Program. Dealer participation is optional, but if every other dealer is selling cars at GM-employee prices, how can any dealer not participate? Also, since 2006, GM has imposed three reductions in dealer margins. In 2009, it had a price increase and a margin reduction at virtually the same time. A 2009 Cobalt 1LT ordered at the beginning of the model year retailed for around $18,000. By the end of the model year, the same car retailed for around $18,600, but it had $200 less markup.

Dealers have long supported GM by stepping up and paying their way. It is important for any manufacturer to realize that by undermining the value of the franchise system and in essence creating policies that discriminate against a large number of dealers, manufacturers reduce dealer satisfaction and customer loyalty. When a local dealership loses the loyalty of some of its customers because of policies created by the factory (such as the system of allocating inventory and incentive programs geared toward larger dealers), customers also have a reduced connection to the division. The next time they trade their car, they may consider a different make, whereas if local dealers had been given an adequate allocation of popular models, they might remain customers for life.

When GM started many of these programs, its market share was well over 40 percent and it was making money. But the imports took away customers one at a time, and domestic manufacturers lost the loyalty of some of their dealers. Suppliers have long considered import companies better to work for than GM and other domestic automakers. Even though excessive union demands, increased competition, and economic problems were to blame for the domestic manufacturers' problems, management problems were also a contributing factor.

Everyone heard GM's Fritz Henderson and Chrysler's Jim Press testify before Congress. They both spoke of how burdensome dealers were on the factory. Press said that the shuttered Chrysler dealers cost Chrysler nearly one billion dollars a year in costs and lost opportunities. Henderson testified that by reducing the dealer network, GM would save over two billion dollars.

An *Automotive News* article reported that, privately, Press was against closing the dealerships and always felt that fewer dealers meant fewer sales (Wernie and Rechtin). In a recent *Dealer Magazine* article on this subject, dealer advocate and automotive industry expert Jim Ziegler said, "There was never a financially sound business reason to terminate any dealer that was profitable, financially solvent, was not out-of-trust, and treated their customers well. But that is exactly what happened." He went on to say, "The majority of forced dealer terminations, Chrysler and GM, were calculated, political, and repercussion-driven" (Ziegler). A July 19, 2010, article on Autoblog.com quoted TARP special inspector general Neil Barofsky as saying the dealer closings weren't "necessarily critical to the manufacturers' viability." Further, he added that closing dealerships would add additional workers to the unemployment ranks "without sufficient consideration of the decisions' broader impact" (Shunk).

GM's first proposed dealer reductions were rejected by the automotive task force because they were not deep enough. The majority of the next round of terminations fell on dealerships in rural markets, where GM and Chrysler had as much as a 10 percent (some pockets are even higher) market-share advantage over the import brands. Barofsky said that a draft report was presented to the Treasury Department; it stated that "relatively little thought" had gone into the reductions. He went on to say that "Treasury ignored one of the few non-Wall Street sources that it consulted, a representative from the nonprofit Center for Automotive Research, who warned that deep cuts could actually do the companies far greater harm than good" (Barofsky). The task force viewed the dealer contracts as one-sided in the dealers' favor and felt that a bankruptcy was a "silver lining" to eliminate dealerships (Rattner). Ironically, the task force recognized that the automakers' size enabled them to dictate payment terms to suppliers and to force dealers to pay for cars before they arrived at the dealerships. The latter was an incentive for the factory to fill dealer lots with of cars. The dictated terms to suppliers and dealers enabled the automakers to hide the automakers' anemic cash-flow position (Rattner).

Regardless of the cash-flow benefit that the dealers provided, the task force recommended deep dealer cuts, and executives at GM and Chrysler were compelled to comply in order to procure the necessary funding to save their respective companies. Some may even consider the task force as misinformed, but without them, regardless of its level of competency, GM never would have gotten the additional $30 billion in funding that was promised when it entered the bankruptcy process. It was also a prime opportunity to frighten or intimidate the "remaining" dealers and force them to upgrade their facilities in accordance with the factories' various image programs.

The pressure on politicians from dealers and consumers concerning the closing of dealerships was so great that Congress passed a law enabling dealers to seek arbitration in an effort to get reinstated. Many dealers signed up for arbitration, and before hearings began, GM voluntarily reinstated over six hundred dealers. Many of the remaining dealers took the higher payouts that GM offered. Less than two hundred ended up going through arbitration, with just over two dozen winning their cases.

Executives expressed how hard these decisions were, but they said they had to be done. A week before Mark LaNeve resigned his post as vice president of GM North America, he was quoted in *Automotive News* as

saying that GM estimated that it had orphaned some three million customers by eliminating these dealerships. He also estimated that because
of the five hundred rural dealerships that were eliminated, GM had orphaned nine hundred thousand customers. In many instances, if these
customers were to continue to purchase GM vehicles, they would have
to drive a couple of hours for routine service on their vehicles (LaReau).

GM had to desert almost one million customers in rural markets,
which it completely dominated. Recent articles in various publications
quoted experts as saying that the gutting of the rural dealer network
was a disastrous move. It still doesn't make sense. Something else that
doesn't make sense is why members of Congress allowed manufacturers
to tell them that dealers were a significant burden to the companies. In
GM's ten-page testimony before Congress, in June 2009, it listed twelve
items that would save the company an estimated two billion dollars.
The following chart summarizes the expected cost savings that GM said
would result from the planned dealer eliminations.

GM's Proposed Dealer Elimination Savings

Item	Savings
1 percent of sticker for advertising	$810 million
Incentives to dealers	$380 million
Standards for Excellence payments	$350 million
New vehicle inspections	$350 million
Factory wholesale floor plan support	$140 million
Fuel fill-ups	$120 million
Local dealer advertising	$200 million
Dealer channel network alignment	$125 million
Sales and service consultants	$40 million
Dealer website and other tools	$30 million
Dealer IT systems and support	$10 million

Many critics contend that the vast majority of these items are not
costs to GM, because either the dealer pays for them or they are the
result of a sale. One president of a state dealer association said that the
items "were the result of a sale and not a reflection of the number of
dealers." It made for good showmanship in justifying the dealer closings,
but it created some tension within the industry.

In the last decade, GM has sold or spun off its interest in Hughes, EDS, Delphi, and GMAC. During the same period, it has lost more than 10 percentage points of market share and billions of dollars. In terms of total auto sales in the United States, 2006 was one of the biggest years in history, but GM lost money. The number of dealers was not an instrumental part of the bankruptcy. Even Ed Whitacre felt that GM may have cut too many dealers. He was quoted as saying, "If you had more good dealers, then you can sell more good cars, and that is what we are in the business of doing. I still believe that it is a much better idea to have more good dealers" (Barofsky).

The Fight for Survival

In 2006, Henderson became GM's chief financial officer. In July 2008, GM announced significant changes in an effort to trim costs and provide the company with sufficient capital to sustain it in any foreseeable crisis. GM also said it was in a better position than Ford because Ford had borrowed against its plants and GM hadn't. In fairness, no one could have foreseen the financial collapse of 2008 and the ensuing credit crisis that forced the government to bail out the auto industry.

Even though GM was losing billions of dollars every year, it still paid a generous dividend into 2008, a decision that cost it one billion dollars a year. This all happened when Henderson was chief financial officer. Part of the reason for the dividend is to support the stock price. Common sense raises the question: If you are losing billions of dollars a year, does it make sense to spend a billion dollars on a dividend?

General Motors and Chrysler were worth saving, though. For decades, politicians had sided with unions, causing an imbalance in the employer/employee relationship, and this was a significant part of the bankruptcy. Poorly negotiated trade agreements often gave foreign competitors advantages, because foreign countries didn't have to deal with unions or environmental regulations.

Finally, just as with Great Northern's bankruptcy, GM management's decisions had a role in charting the course that led to the ultimate failure of the corporation. The good news is that changes made during the painful bankruptcy have led to a reinvigorated General Motors. The passion for product has never been stronger. GM's CFO, Dan Ammann, was quoted in *Automotive News* as saying, "If you don't have a natural interest in the business of designing and building cars, it's not going to work" (Colias, "CFO Says GM..."). GM already had great products, but new products in the pipeline have created excitement in the press and with consumers. In 2013, proof of the success can be found in increased sales and fifteen straight quarters of profitability since emerging from bankruptcy.

Chapter Six

The Real War

America is fighting wars and rumors of wars. We have a traditional war in the Middle East, which reportedly is part of the War on Terror, but we also have diversionary wars like the war on poverty, the war on drugs, the war on illegal immigration, and many more. We are winning some of these wars and loosing others, but the war that we are ignoring is the war for America's future. America is being attacked on multiple fronts by big government, big labor, and big business. These internal forces sometimes deliberately undermine our system, and in other cases the harm is unknowingly and unintentionally applied by decent citizens.

The Casualties of War

Evidence of these attacks can be found in the histories of GNP and GM. Two strong powerful companies were attacked and badgered to the point where each became unable to continue. Most of the original GNP assets in Millinocket have been removed, and GM was only able to re-structure because of a $50 billion bailout from the federal government.

GNP had enormous competitive advantages in Maine. It had the largest privately owned hydroelectric system in the country, two million acres of land, a state-of-the-art research and development center, and an incredible apprentice training program. Wave upon wave of attacks from big government and big labor provided enough incremental costs that big business decided not to invest in its Maine operations.

The attacks from the state were in the form of burdensome regulations, uncompetitive taxes, and obstructionist polices. On at least one occasion, GNP tried to invest in a technology that would have eliminated the need for four hundred and thirty-eight thousand barrels of oil per year, but environmental factions within the state deliberately thwarted the investment. All of these factors added significant incremental cost to doing business.

Compounding a hostile state was pressure from labor. While labor was never hostile, generous compensation packages and stringent work rules made the cost of labor measurably higher in Maine verses GNN's southern operations. Eventually, the local unions made significant compensation concessions and amended work rules, but it didn't prevent the Millinocket mill from being razed.

The poor business climate in Maine prevented GNN from making necessary investments in Maine. When investments were scheduled in the late 1990s, a hostile Wall Street takeover stopped the investment. Many of the owners since the initial takeover have cannibalized operations, leaving little for a future economy.

Many of the same big-government, big-labor, and big-business factors contributed to an uncompetitive situation that forced GM into bankruptcy. Big government's siding with big labor combined with Wall Street's pressure to keep the money flowing forced GM into very poor labor contracts, which made GM's cost of production significantly higher than that incurred by foreign competitors who had non-union manufacturing facilities. In 2008, government meddling and Wall Street greed caused the worst financial collapse since the Great Depression. The collapse forced GM into bankruptcy and to seek a $50 billion bailout.

The tragic economic collapses of the Magic City and General Motors offer striking lessons. There are scary similarities between the path this country has taken and where the Magic City and GM have already been. But it is not too late to set things aright. The solutions are not easy, nor will they be popular, but, given these two case studies, they are necessary.

The lessons may seem patently obvious, but they have to be stated, because it appears that some of them have been lost to our own arrogance.

Many of them could be combined into a one-word summation—greed—while others could be attributed to a lack of foresight. Some of them don't in themselves point to a solution, but they do provide us with a baseline for future decision making.

Regardless of where they come from, delays, distractions, and uncertainty kill entrepreneurial spirit. The events of the last several years have proven that despite trillions of dollars of stimulus, when businesses are barraged with new regulations and uncertainty, they don't expand and invest. America's economic recovery hinges on government learning and understanding this principle.

Sam Walton, the founder of Wal-Mart, was one of the greatest retail visionaries of the last century. He started with one store and continued to expand with a relatively simple concept and he never lost touch with the stores and his customers. He regularly visited the stores and talked to the employees to get their feedback. Walton said that Wal-Mart got big because it thought like a small company (Walton and Huey).

The Sacrificial Lamb

Americans in general have a misconception of how business works. Businesspeople are often characterized as greedy, seeking profits over everything else. Many big businesses can seem that way, but the average entrepreneur is more of an artist than a greedster. There is a need for big businesses and venture-capital firms, because not all of them are evil. The economies of scale that can be achieved with a large organization provide enormous benefit to the economy.

Most big businesses started out as small businesses. Many entrepreneurs, while concerned about profits, are driven with passion, just as an artist is driven to create a masterpiece. To the entrepreneur, the business is the canvas, and it becomes the manifestation of a vision. Many small-business owners work harder and longer hours for less money than they would for someone else, but it is their vision and passion that drive their efforts. In the case of GNP and GM, when the environment was conducive, entrepreneurs invested in a vision, and history was made.

Creating a business isn't a chicken-or-egg thing; a positive business climate has to exist. A business climate is made up of two parts. One is government regulations, and the other is the marketplace. The marketplace has two parts: one is the consumer's willingness to purchase a given product or service, and the other is the amount of competition within that industry. When the sum total of the parts of the business climate is positive, it inspires people with vision and passion, and they seek and attract the necessary capital to start a business.

When a business attracts necessary capital, it has to organize the operation and get everyone working together to maximize efficiency. In the cases of GNP and GM, this is the process that led to success. That success translated to prosperity for the investors, the workers, and the people in the surrounding communities.

In both examples, long-term success came from continued reinvestment, innovation, and various forms of diversification or vertical integration. This kept the companies ahead of their competitors. Another important factor in the long-term success of GNP and GM was stability. Regulatory stability, market stability, and organizational stability are necessary for an organization to continue to attract investment in its operations.

When any of these conditions becomes compromised, the business and the community in which it is located are extremely vulnerable. For GNP, the conditions in both cases eroded, and the company directed necessary capital to locations that would provide a better return on investment. The lack of investment in the Maine mills eventually made them uncompetitive and unprofitable. In the case of GM, a variety of factors including, burdensome labor contracts and exorbitant health-care costs contributed to its becoming so saddled with debt that banks wouldn't lend it any more money. The debt made its cost basis per car too high to sustain operations. The ensuing cash-flow problem forced it into bankruptcy.

The Battle with Big Business

Most companies are run by good people, but the "Wall Street mandate" for short-term profits threatens the long-term mission of most companies, which is to provide the maximum benefit to the maximum number of people and thereby earn a profit. Not everything that big government, big labor, and big business does is harmful to the country. Some things can only be done by a large organization, but there are definite patterns that undermine America's foundation.

Insofar as big business is concerned, much of the battle can be blamed on shortsighted decisions, and these are related to executive compensation. Not all companies reward executives with overly generous compensation packages, but many do. In many large companies, there is no ownership, because in some instances the chief executive officer (CEO) and other top executives have short five-year tenures (Griffin).

These executives tend to focus primarily on the short-term stock price (Griffin). One former executive said that there are very few CEOs who run large corporations as if they are going to pass the company over to their sons. Imagine it this way: There are two people and each buys a car; one of them cares for it with the expectation of giving it to his son when it is paid for (slightly higher maintenance cost), and the other person does only enough maintenance to make the car last until it is paid for (lower maintenance cost). Given the opportunity, which car would you buy when it was paid for? Which car has the best long-term value? The same applies to a business. Short-term cost savings can boost the stock price for a period of time, but, eventually, as in the case of GNP, the company can suffer a competitive disadvantage due to a lack of investment.

Other short-term tactics are to reduce maintenance services, product features, and advertising for a temporary boost in profits. These methods reduce long-term profits, because reduced maintenance only delays the inevitable and often results in deferred costs. If someone doesn't want to spend thirty-five dollars for an oil change and decides to simply add a quart when needed, then he or she may get sixty or seventy thousand miles from a five-thousand-dollar engine—instead of a hundred and fifty thousand or two hundred thousand miles, with proper maintenance.

Reducing product features or cheapening the product by moving production offshore can reduce perceived value, quality, and alienate customers. The result of this is reduced brand loyalty. Reduced loyalty eventually leads to lower long-term sales and profits. There is no need for an expensive study on this issue; it is simply a fact that if a product has less perceived value or appeal, then customers purchase less of the product (or the product has to be sold at a lower price), and profits decline.

One of the ways to shift executives' thinking to a longer time frame is by reforming the way executives are paid. I'm not saying executives are overpaid, but the way in which their compensation is derived is part of the problem. The *Wall Street Journal* had a great article on the subject of executive compensation. The article listed several ways to have executives run companies correctly. One of the ways was to make executives keep their stock for a longer period of time after they retire. Another was to base compensation on the level of debt as well as the stock price. The theory here is that it will help the company's stock price by reducing excessive risk taking and by aligning management's interests with creditors' interests instead of focusing on the stockholders' interests alone (Edmans).

The focus on this quarter's or next quarter's stock price means that, in essence, Wall Street is running large companies. Wall Street analysts' quarterly phone calls with companies primarily focus on that quarter's profits and the direction of the company over the next couple of quarters (Griffin). If a company misses a target, or exceeds a target but the direction for the next quarter is negative, the stock market price can have a disproportionately negative reaction. Tom Griffin feels that the tendency for Wall Street is to very often frown on capital investment, because it is a drag on the short-term value of the stock. Furthermore, the pressure to "keep the money flowing" pushes companies into poor union contracts (Griffin). Rather than tough it out and negotiate a contract that would allow a company to be competitive in a global marketplace, companies historically entered negotiations with the attitude that they were going to give the unions as little as possible so long as the workers kept working. Without proper capital investment and competitive union contracts, the long-term value of the company is sacrificed for the benefit of the near-term stock price.

Therefore, depending on how the executives' compensation is formulated, it may behoove an executive to delay necessary capital improvements that would strengthen long-term competitiveness but would weaken short-term stock values. A major capital improvement has the potential to reduce operating cash, increase debt, and lower short-term profits due to increased depreciation.

Another disadvantage with paying executives based upon "today's performance" is that an executive could also significantly increase debt on risky investments whose long-term sustainability is questionable. It could be adding extra capacity for a product that could be obsolete in a few years. A company could purchase assets that provide a brief boost to revenues and profit but which will require extensive renovations and expense a few years later.

My father summarizes the perils of short-term thinking and corner cutting by saying, "You cannot save your way into a profit." Great Northern and its subsequent owners virtually saved themselves out of existence. It wasn't the local managers' fault. They constantly proposed budgets with large capital investments, but those proposals were often cut by corporate headquarters. In some instances, a corporation can save itself out of business.

The Battle with Big Labor

It is hard to conceive that big labor would have policies that harm the middle class, but it shares part of the blame for the increased pressures on the middle class. Unions are not intentionally harmful, but the past actions of many unions decreased the long-term well-being of their members. When unions were shutting down factories one after another from the 1950s into the 1980s, this created an environment in which companies would find it lucrative to make investments in right-to-work states or to move operations to countries like Mexico and China.

Another way the unions have hampered progress is through work rules. It was common for some union shops to have rules so specific that if someone other than an electrician changed a light bulb, a member of the electricians' union could file a grievance. Rules such as this make it very expensive to operate a business.

Unions have been so focused on union rights and member benefits that they lost sight of the big picture. The middle class did well during those years, but as the economy became increasingly global, compensation packages and work rules became unsustainable. Unfortunately for scores of communities, factories relocated to areas that had lower labor costs before the unions agreed to easier terms. By the time unions started to relax work rules and amend pay and benefit packages, it was too late. The once-prosperous factories and communities became modern-day ghost towns. Much of the once-prosperous middle class was forced into the unemployment lines. The unions in Millinocket and East Millinocket amended work rules and compensation levels several times in an effort to keep their jobs, but the Millinocket mill was bulldozed anyway.

The Battle with Big Government

The third threat to our future is the government itself. Ephesians 6:12 (King James Version) summarizes it well by stating, *"For we wrestle not against flesh and blood, but against principalities, against powers, against the rulers of the darkness of this world, against spiritual wickedness in high places."* Parts of the government are so focused on self-preservation and growth that their proponents are oblivious to the complete and utter dismantling of the middle class, small businesses, and hometown America. Some of the blame could be assigned to pandering politicians seeking the equivalent of life-long appointments to elected positions.

All of the key stressors that caused the demise of the Millinocket paper mill and the bankruptcy of GM are being expanded at an alarming rate. The national economy is going to suffer the same fate as the Katahdin region. Two of the three towns that comprise the Katahdin region are on a trajectory toward bankruptcy. As I am rewriting this chapter in 2013, East Millinocket is debating on whether to spend several million dollars on necessary maintenance on its high school, but at the same time, the town's projected enrollments and revenue are expected to decline. Millinocket announced in June of 2013 that it had a budget gap of $3 million to $4.5 million, and because it was not collecting a sufficient amount of its outstanding tax bills, its bank considered Millinocket a high risk for a tax-anticipation note (a short-term loan to fund the town until its next year's tax revenue starts).

Just because this is America, it does not mean that states or the entire nation is immune to total economic collapse. Other countries—such as Mexico, the former Union of Soviet Socialist Republics, and countries in the European Union, including Greece—have had economic collapses. These countries, and, unless it changes, the United States, have seen almost all of the same warning signs as GNP and GM.

Regulations, like the ones that thwarted GNP, are being expanded on a national basis. Unsustainable compensation packages, like the ones that burdened GM, for some government employees are contributing to budget deficits. Entitlement programs, like Social Security and Medicare, are paying out more than they are taking in. Finally, a mountain of crippling debt is setting the stage for massive amounts of inflation. When federal and state debt becomes so enormous, it will be deemed high risk, just like Millinocket's debt and the cost of the debt will increase in accordance with the perceived risk.

In order for the federal government to service its debt, it will have two options. One, it will virtually eliminate the US military, or, two, it will print more money. The second is the more likely choice, but the consequence of printing too much money is that it produces hyperinflation. In post-World War I Germany, the cost of a loaf of bread was so much that it took a wheelbarrow-load of money to purchase a loaf of bread.

The battle against big government is going to have to be fought in the voting booths, because well-intentioned and often unqualified politicians seeking positive headlines often choose what is popular over what is necessary. A great example can be found in the One Hundred Twelfth Congress. April 29, 2012, marked the third anniversary since the US Senate passed a budget. Worse than that, the federal debt ceiling and tax laws have been extended for months instead of years. Three key pieces of the economy, whose stability is necessary for businesses to plan investments, have been kicked around by politicians as if they don't matter.

Congress and government agencies have buried businesses with tidal waves of shifting regulations. One of the keys to business investment is stability, and when the government constantly changes the rules of the game via regulations, businesses withhold investment dollars or choose to place them in other places. Changing regulations are a constant distraction that siphon off money and energy to maintain compliance.

As an example, Royal Dutch Shell spent $4.5 billion over the last seven years for leases and permissions to drill exploratory oil wells off the coast of Alaska. The company obtained numerous approvals from the Obama administration, but last-minute challenges forced the company to scale back its proposal for 2012 (Eilperin and Mufson). Shell has invested billions and has not even turned a drill. Every time a challenge to permits is issued, it delays the project and the costs go up.

Environmental groups are synonymous with big government. The stronger the environmental groups get, the more powerful and onerous the government becomes. It is all in the name of control and power. These groups and the government want power and control, because power and control is money. Money is how they make their living. If local governments and businesses have control, then the larger government agencies are not needed. Environmentalism has been the leading force in a massive shift of power from local control to a more centralized control.

When businesses and communities lose control of the ability to invest, then their future falls victim to the political whims of the central government. The Millinocket and East Millinocket mills lost not only the ability to control their destiny within the company but also within the web of government regulations. It was that loss of control that was a major factor in the mills' inability to attract enough capital improvements to ensure their long-term viability.

Environmental groups were raising money as far away as California to defeat the Big A dam project. If politicians and environmental groups continue to dupe the American public with fear mongering, then the entire nation will be subjected to the dictates of an international bureaucracy that will determine the future of America's economy.

The motives behind many of the environmental groups are suspicious at best. Former Sierra Club executive Ron Arnold has written several books on the subject, and he explains in his chapter titled "How Runaway Environmentalism is Wrecking America" in the book *Trashing the Economy*. Arnold shows the budgets and pet projects of national environmental groups. As he dissects the motives behind the environmental groups, their political agenda is revealed. Arnold provides numerous examples of how environmental groups bully and exaggerate to achieve their dubious motives.

You only have to watch an interview of someone who questions man's involvement in global warming to see an example of environmental bullying. Anyone who publicly questions global warming is criticized. The science behind man's involvement in global warming or climate change is not 100-percent conclusive. Professor Phil Jones, the climatologist who was director of the University of East Anglia's Climate Research Unit, told the British Broadcasting Corporation (BBC) that there had been no statistically significant warming in the last fifteen years. Professor Jones also said that it is possible that the Medieval Warm Period was possibly warmer than it is now, which throws into question mankind's involvement in global warming and climate change (Petre). Furthermore, the raw data that supported the hockey-stick-shaped rise in global temperatures had turned up missing, and the ensuing controversy was called "Climategate."

What's worse is that the political winds of global warming pose a sovereignty issue for America. Most nations signed a treaty called the Kyoto Protocol. Kyoto was designed to reduce greenhouse gas emissions by approximately 5 percent from 1990 levels. It mandated that the United States reduce its greenhouse gas emissions by 7 percent from the 1990 levels, while developing countries like China and India were exempt, and Russia's levels were capped at the 1990 levels (CBC News, 2007). The United States never signed it, because it was going to be a major threat to the US economy.

CBC reported that the cuts were to take place over a five-year period, from 2008 to 2012. I found it interesting that the price of crude oil increased over 51 percent in just seven months in 2008. The massive increase in oil prices exacerbated a weak financial market, and the entire world (perhaps with the exception of China and India) was drawn into the deepest recession since the Great Depression. Five years later, the world economy remains depressed.

Politicians often talk about using cap-and-trade rules to lower greenhouse gases. Cap-and-trade is a system whereby a governmental agency sets emission limits and companies are able to either:

- Lower emissions beyond the cap and sell credits to companies that cannot meet the levels or
- Purchase credits.

If cap-and-trade is applied internationally, then an international agency will have to oversee the implementation of geographical pollution limits and develop a mechanism through which companies and maybe even countries can swap pollution credits.

There are powers that want the United States to participate in some type of Kyoto-style treaty. The danger is that handing over that much of the US economy to an international group would have the same effects on the economy as the environmental movement has had in Maine. Air and water quality is important, but enormous progress has been made already. And constantly changing the rules for minor improvements has a major impact on the ability of companies and small communities to adapt. This is especially troubling when a company in another nation doesn't have to abide by the same rules. It creates an imbalance that drains one area that would have had effective pollution control and shifts economic activity to another area with no pollution control.

If the United States hands a large part of its economy to an international bureaucracy, it would have a devastating effect on America. It would have the same effect that the Katahdin region experienced every time control was taken from local management at GNP. Whether control was taken by corporate headquarters or by the government, the community and the local mills were not able to compete with regions that had lower costs. The disparity meant the Maine mills failed to attract the necessary capital investments to profitably compete in the long term.

For decades, Maine entrepreneurs were under attack from the state. The state and environmental groups come to the people as friends promising to help, but end up "frustrating plans" just like the opposition to those who were rebuilding the Temple in Ezra Chapter 4. Ezra 4:4-5 states, "*Then the people of the land weakened the hands of the people of Judah, and troubled them in the building, and hired counselors against them, to frustrate their purpose...*" Increased regulations, more mandates, and higher taxes poisoned the business climate. The US government has been creating the same atmosphere that crippled Maine. A barrage of new regulations, like the Dodd-Frank Wall Street Reform and Consumer Protection Act and the Affordable Health Care Act, have prompted businesses in America to scramble to maintain compliance, and they are scared because of an uncertain future. And at the same time that the economy is languishing, President Obama criticizes businesses. He discounted individual achievement when he said that businesses couldn't have been built without the help of the government. This shows the same hostile attitude that the state of Maine has had.

What so many politicians fail to realize is that without profit, the government wouldn't have any tax revenue to build the roads. Without profit, businesses wouldn't invest and hire employees. Without profit, businesses cannot operate, and when businesses stop operating, the economy stops. Why would people in their right mind expose themselves in this litigious environment without the hope of a profit?

Whether the attacks on our future come from an international bureaucracy or from the US government, the way control is popularized is by promising to plunder the rich for the sake of the poor. It is a popular theme. The problem is that when the profit motive is vilified, the cycle stops.

As GNP's mills became less profitable, the company started downsizing. The continued downsizing without new investment was a factor in the mills' being less competitive (Doody). The downsizing caused the fixed costs to be distributed among fewer and fewer productive assets and as a result contributed to less profitability. The lack of modernization and the constant contraction of the region's largest employer was devastating. Decades of overbearing control from the state played a key role in the collapse. If Americans continue to embrace (vote for) the demigods of defeat, then our future can be best summarized by Psalms 49:20, which states, "*Man that is in honor, and understandeth not, is like the beasts that perish.*"

Chapter Seven

Winning the Future

A large number of big businesses in America have been downsizing in recent years. The federal government's debt is increasing at an alarming rate, Social Security and Medicare are paying out more than they are taking in, an increasing number of cities and counties are filing for bankruptcy, and some states are on the verge of bankruptcy. As an example, in July of 2013, the city of Detroit, Michigan, filed for Chapter 9 bankruptcy protection. At the time of filing, it was the largest US city to file for bankruptcy. Detroit once had a population of approximately 1.7 million and was one of the most prosperous cities in the world. A generation later, the city, which epitomized big government, big labor, and big business, had a population of only 700,000 and debt of about $18 billion. A September 2013 drive through Detroit reveals an economically depressed city that has an eerie and ominous presence, because of its former glory. In large sections of the city it is easier to count the occupied buildings, because the vacant ones are so numerous. It is easier to count the whole panes of glass in the vacant buildings than to count the broken ones. The once prosperous city is now plagued with poverty.

Detroit is a magnification of too many of America's small towns. Therefore, Americans cannot count on the government or most big businesses to fix the problems in small-town America. Americans need to have a way to win in the future. When the economy stagnates and the future appears uncertain, Americans need to look in the mirror—and beyond—for help.

When considering how to win the future, it is necessary to realize that there is something simply beyond money and pleasures. When describing the value of wealth and pleasures, Ecclesiastes 2:11 states, "*Then I looked on all the works that my hands had wrought, and on the labor that I had labored to do: and, behold, all was vanity and vexation of spirit, and there was no profit under the sun.*" Psalms 118:8-9 states, "*It is better to trust in the Lord than to put confidence in man. It is better to trust in the Lord than to put confidence in princes.*" Americans should remember the founding fathers and consider God when making plans. The Declaration of Independence has four direct references to God, and the Constitution is signed, "In the year of our Lord."

An essential first step in success is to rely more on God and less on government. It is unreasonable to expect government to fix what it broke in the first place. What drives a successful nation is the unwavering faith that if God is with you, no one can stand against you. Hebrews 11:1 describes faith by stating, "*Now faith is the substance of things hoped for, the evidence of things not seen.*" With faith, people, businesses, and nations grow and expand; without faith, there is no vision, and that leads to death.

If money and power are the only motivators, the system breaks down. There is nothing wrong with being rich or powerful; it should be encouraged, if it glorifies God. Keeping God in the picture forces us to deal fairly with others and to consider their needs. That is the first step in turning the country around. Success is a long road with many steps, but every small community, small business, and individual has the opportunity.

A Vision, Enthusiasm, and a Plan

Whether it is an individual or a small community, the path to success is similar to the elements of a successful business. People and communities need to have a vision beyond letting the government do things for them. Proverbs 29:18 states, "*Where there is no vision, the people perish: But he that keepeth the law, happy is he.*" In this instance, the word "vision" relates to "spiritual vision." It could also be said that where there is no economic vision, the economy perishes.

Given its financial condition, the only thing the government can afford to do is to get out of the way of entrepreneurs and small communities. One of the biggest problems is that too many people and small communities lack vision. With no vision, there cannot be any path to winning the future. Former General Motors CEO Fritz Henderson was fired in 2009, because, despite his extensive knowledge of the global automobile industry, the board of directors lost confidence in his ability to form a clear vision for the company (Colias).

The first step in creating a plan is to ask three questions:

1. Where am I?
2. Where do I want to be?
3. How do I get there?

A sober look at present circumstances enables people to be thankful for what they do have. In fact, I have found it beneficial to think of three or four things that I'm truly thankful for every night. That simple exercise helps to reduce the stumbling block of bitterness. It also allows me to better strategize how I can improve.

If people don't know what they actually have, then they cannot develop an accurate vision. After answering the first question, a vision develops from the second question: "Where do I want to be?" The final question, "How do I get there?" leads to a plan of action.

It is important to keep plans flexible. Circumstances change, and if the plan isn't adapted to the change, failure could be the result. Being stubborn and inflexible with a plan often ends in higher costs and more hassles. Sometimes it is necessary to stick to a plan. Shopping locally and buying products that are made in America would be perfect examples of elements of a plan that should remain constant.

Part of any individual's or small community's plan needs to include the elements of buying products locally and buying American-made products. The argument against buying locally is often, "I can buy it cheaper somewhere else." Maybe you can, maybe you can't, but the important thing to remember is that a dollar spent in a local community circulates in that community up to seven times. In other words, one dollar of spending has a seven-dollar impact on the local economy. It increases the likelihood that you will receive some measure of return on the purchase as the dollar recirculates.

Local loyalty is the only way that a small community can truly grow its retail and economic base. If the people in a small town are not willing to help themselves, then why should anyone else invest in that community? Purchasing products locally, even if they cost a little extra, enables more stores to remain open and to expand and hire more employees. When money is siphoned out of town, the local shops often go out of business or reduce employment levels. If enough economic outflow occurs, a community can develop significant economic problems.

I like to use the Amish in Smyrna, Maine, as an example of how shopping locally works. The Amish live in close-knit communities that are self-supporting. In the case of Smyrna, the Amish have a shed-building business, a general store, and other enterprises. On paper, it makes little sense to move to northern Maine to open a shed-building business and a general store, but both enterprises are busy and appear to be doing well. The key is local support.

A different type of example shows how shopping locally has reciprocal value. I know of two parts stores: one is a locally-owned franchise of a national firm, and the other is owned by a national chain. The owner of the locally-owned store purchases and maintains vehicles at the local dealership, whereas the nationally-owned store has a national contract and purchases and maintains vehicles through a fleet service. Guess which store has twice the local dealer's business each and every month? By pulling control away from the local managers, the national company alienated its local customer base.

Shopping locally can be extended to include a buy-American movement. Maine has lost thousands of quality manufacturing jobs and the United States has lost millions, because consumers have chosen to purchase cheaper imports. Big businesses get blamed for being greedy, and that is partially true, but what about the consumers who, when provided with a choice, tell the merchant that they want to buy the less expensive alternative—even though it may mean that a fellow American may lose his or her job?

People in small communities everywhere need to take these basic elements and add to them. People also need to be enthusiastic in their endeavors. Shopping locally, buying American, and other elements of the plan should become a passion. If there is no passion, the plan will founder. Every plan is the result of a vision, and passion not only puts the plan into action, it keeps the plan going.

Organization and Stability

Individuals, small businesses, and small towns have the same need for organization and stability as large enterprises. An unorganized and unstable household fails to reach its maximum potential. Disorganization wastes time, and the instability in rules, desires, and goals causes constant distractions. We've all seen houses with numerous projects in progress and none finished. Projects are expensive to start, and unfinished projects detract from a home's value. When students change their desires in college, that usually requires changing a major, and that often extends the length of time it takes to graduate and thus increases the cost of their education.

Small communities and small businesses face the same difficulties. When a small town has constant shifts in focus, it scares off investors, who fear that the town's changing attitudes could cause expensive policy shifts. Likewise with small businesses that follow the marketing gimmick of the week or have inconsistent hours often alienate consumers.

A way to increase organization and stability is to make goals and plans specific and clear. Using shopping lists and projects-to-do lists helps to increase efficiency and reduce wasted time. As personal efficiency increases, it becomes easier to manage personal finance.

Personal Finance

Whether for a business or an individual, wealth is built over a lifetime and with a goal in mind. True monetary wealth rarely comes from gambling. In other words, there are few, if any, shortcuts on the road to financial independence. Hard work, discipline, and direction are key ingredients in sound financial planning.

In the fall of 2011, Maine's Governor, Paul LePage, held a Jobs Summit for business leaders at Husson University. His goal was to find out what the state could do to create an environment that would encourage businesses to hire more people. Groups of approximately thirty business leaders at a time met with the governor in closed-door meetings. In one of the closed-door meetings, I heard one business leader describe an epidemic that is weighing on the economy: an alarming number of young people have damaged credit. The problem, as he described it, was that most public schools fail to teach personal finance. High school students are forced to take liberal arts classes instead of learning the fundamentals of personal finance.

The lack of financial education has led to a crisis whereby money controls people instead of people controlling money. One ominous sign that precipitated the great financial crash of 2008 was the savings rate in the United States in 2005–2006. In 2005, the savings rate was a negative 0.5 percent, which was the lowest savings rate since 1933 (Associated

Press, 2006). The savings rate dipped even lower, to a negative 1 percent, in 2006 (Associated Press, 2007). The low savings rate was at the peak of the housing boom. Rapidly increasing home values created a false sense of security in some consumers and financial experts. When fuel and food prices skyrocketed in 2008, there was little savings available to cover the increased costs.

In 2010, the Employee Benefit Research Institute's Retirement Confidence Survey reported that 27 percent of the working population had less than one thousand dollars in savings (not including housing and defined benefit plans). According to the US Census Bureau's employment statistics from 2005 to 2009, there were approximately 153 million Americans in the labor force. This means that over 41 million American workers (27 percent of 153 million) are one minor mishap (or oil shock) away from a financial crisis. The economic implication of that many Americans having a financial crisis at the same time is frightening.

The way to create a new America is to show all Americans how to control money. Saving requires planning and discipline. The financial plan needs to mirror an individual's goals and vision. Every purchase has to be compared with a person's goals by way of this question: Does this complement my long-term goals, or does it detract from them? Financial distractions are as deadly to individuals as they are to business.

Some financial distractions are unavoidable—the washing machine goes on the fritz or the oven stops working. But there are many small distractions that most people deliberately engage in but whose long-term financial impact they don't realize. I call it the Franklin Financial Effect. One of America's greatest statesmen, Benjamin Franklin, is credited with saying, "Beware of little expenses, as a small leak will sink a great ship." In planning for retirement, the focus of many financial experts is on big-ticket items, but the total of purchasing small distractions over a lifetime overshadows the single "big" purchases that most Americans make.

The following table illustrates the Franklin Financial Effect. The prices in the table are approximate averages and do not reflect inflation (prices may vary by market), and the thirty-five-year figure includes putting the yearly cost of the distraction in an investment account at 8 percent compound interest.

Item	Yearly Cost	35 Yr. Future Value
Coffee: 1 per work day (260) @ $1.38	$ 360.00	$ 62,034.00
Bottled Water/Soda: 1 per day (365) @ $1.00	$ 365.00	$ 62,895.00
Weekday Lunch: Incremental daily cost Vs. brown bagging $5.00 per work day (265)	$1,300.00	$224,011.00
Vending Machine Snack: 1 per work day (260) @ $1.00	$ 260.00	$ 44,802.00
Interest on credit cards: average carried balance of $3,500 @ 14%	$ 490.00	$ 84,435.00
Unused Gym Memberships, Phone Minutes Cable Channels etc.: $25.00 per month	$ 300.00	$ 51,695.00
Lottery/scratch Tickets: 3 per week @ $1.00	$ 156.00	$ 26,881.00
Smoking: 1 pack per day (365) @ $5.00	$1,825.00	$314,428.00
Total	**$5,056.00**	**$871,181.00**

Consumers pay a premium for the convenience of pre-prepared meals. They also pay a premium for the convenience of being able to pay insurance premiums monthly rather than yearly, because many insurance companies charge a fee of up to five to ten dollars a month for monthly billing. Also, raising a deductible can easily lower most insurance premiums over one hundred dollars a year. By purchasing fewer pre-prepared foods, having higher insurance deductibles, and paying insurance premiums in full rather than monthly, people can save thousands of dollars over thirty-five years.

There are almost endless ways to save small amounts of money, and those small amounts of money add up over time. I personally don't like budgets, but some people lack the discipline to base purchases on their long-term goals, so they need to use budgets.

Regardless of whether one uses a budget, a major financial pitfall for most Americans is credit cards. It is very difficult for average people to save money if they frequently use credit cards, and therefore credit and debit cards should only be used for emergencies. Families need to get in the habit of sitting down and determining monthly obligations (which should include savings and tithes) in relation to income. That money should be set aside first, and the remainder is discretionary. The beautiful thing about using cash is that when your wallet is empty, you are done spending for the week. In a short amount of time, every purchase is scrutinized in relation to long-term needs and goals.

This process applies to small communities as well as to families. When millions of Americans and small communities achieve control over their finances, that gives them power over their future. America was built by small communities, small businesses, and individuals succeeding in spite of all circumstances. A proper financial education and implementation can reinvigorate America.

Innovation and Investment

Three key elements of any business's success are innovation, investment, and reinvestment in the operation. Individuals need to do the same thing. It is often said that "necessity is the mother of all invention," and Americans have led the world by asking "why not?" instead of "why?" When people ask why not, they think of a better way and develop a plan to get there, and that is how innovation occurs.

The process is continued by investment. People need to invest in themselves just like businesses need to. When the Berkshire Hathaway CEO and financial investment guru Warren Buffett was asked what type of investments people should make in times of high inflation, he said that people should invest in themselves. In other words, by improving existing skills and knowledge and learning new skills and trades, people can solidify or even improve their standing in an uncertain economy.

Never Give In

Individuals who have been the victims of government obstructionism, big-business downsizing, or big labor's "it isn't our fault" shouldn't get discouraged. It will be extremely difficult, but they should view unfortunate circumstances as an opportunity to improve themselves or their business. The second that people decide that they cannot succeed, they are right.

When England stood virtually alone against Nazi Germany, it was the courage, vision, and unwavering faith in God of one man that encouraged and rallied the free world. In a 1940 London speech, Winston Churchill said, "Remember that we shall never stop, never weary, and never give in" (Churchill). At one point, the military resources in England were so scarce that soldiers were training with broom sticks, but Churchill knew that "in God's good time" Germany would be defeated.

I have personally seen businesses that have endured and remained profitable beyond all the rules of business. Even in the face of a rapidly declining population, with unemployment at 30 percent, and with an uncertain future, some businesses in Millinocket remained profitable. I had the privilege of being part of such a business. Looking back at that crisis, I can only give thanks for getting through it. Challenges such as these help forge strength and a can-do attitude that provides the foundation for overcoming future obstacles.

If we go back to the story of Job, after he lost everything, including his health, he cursed the day of his birth—but never lost his faith. In the end, Job ended up with more than what Satan had taken from him. Business usually works the same way. If individuals, businesses, and communities use trials as opportunities to learn, improve, and diversify, they will probably emerge from the crisis stronger and in a better position to succeed. That doesn't mean that it will be easy, because it will not be. When people think that they cannot push any harder, they'll have to dig in and push anyway. When they don't have enough hours in the day to complete the increased workload, they'll have to make the hours.

Tragedy in all forms also gives us the opportunity to realize where we should put our faith. Putting faith in the government, in a union, or in big business is a waste of time and energy. During the darkest days of the Great Northern bankruptcy, there was a tremendous amount of pain and uncertainty. Then one afternoon, I looked out my office window toward the closed mill and I saw a rainbow. At that moment, I knew that we were going to be all right. By putting one's faith in the correct place and refusing to give up, people can and will be victorious, no matter what the odds.

I could not have continued to move forward in those dark days had it not been for my faith. Throughout that period, there were too many days when I didn't have a logical reason to get up in the morning, but I continued to fight. I had friends who told me on more than one occasion that the cause was lost and we were wasting our time. But God had a different plan for my family and me.

I have seen the impossible happen in business, because I've lived it. Working from seven a.m. to midnight was sometimes necessary, but the ability and willingness to work that many hours came from the Lord. When I look back at those dark days, I can see how the Lord placed the right people in the right place at exactly the right time to see our business through the turmoil.

Americans should find comfort in knowing that no man's plans can stand against God's plans. God promises to prosper the righteous even in the desert. This doesn't mean that people always get their way, but the people who are faithful to God can overcome impossible circumstances.

Epilogue

The day this manuscript was completed, January 23, 2014, its release was delayed because of an announcement from the new Great Northern Paper Company that it would be halting paper production at the East Millinocket facility for up to sixteen weeks. During this time, employees are scheduled to work, for sixty days, on known maintenance issues and to find ways to improve energy efficiency. All through the curtailment, management will be working to create a new business plan.

In an interview, company spokesman Scott Tranchemontagne stated that the future for GNP employees would be uncertain until the business plan was completed. The company is looking for solutions to its high-operational costs and the comparatively low price of paper. Sources familiar with the situation stated that the relatively high prices for: electricity, wood, and natural gas are factors in the decision. It is ironic that in the 1970s and 1980s, GNN also cited energy and wood costs as being significant factors in determining the allocation of capital investments. The *Bangor Daily News* reported that Governor LePage's administration was going to work with GNP to put them in the position of long-term success. The governor's spokeswoman was quick to stress the burden of high electricity costs and that Governor Lepage has long advocated policies to reduce electricity costs for all Mainers.

Even though some news reports said the company was behind in its obligations to suppliers, informants tell me that GNP ran a successful paper trial (a large sample of paper for a printer to test) less than a week before the announced stoppage. The trial grade of paper had never been produced in the East Millinocket mill, but it was worth the effort, because the new grade reportedly sells for a much higher price than many other grades of paper. This relates to the second part of GNP's reported problem – that paper prices are too low.

News reports also stated that because of price instability, GNP would be stopping the transition to natural gas. GNP had recently considered adding a natural gas boiler (in addition to East's existing bark boiler) to increase its steam output, thus allowing them to bring a second paper machine online. A second paper machine would allow fixed overhead to be divided between two machines instead of one, thereby lowering the fixed overhead cost per machine. However, reports of fluctuating natural gas prices allegedly thwarted completion of the plan.

GNP's parent company, Cate Street Capital, reached an agreement with Governor LePage to allow GNP to sell its excess electricity. Selling electricity is not a new concept to the mills, but changes in Maine State law had to be made in order to allow it. Representative Steve Stanley submitted an emergency bill to allow the practice. Cate Street hopes that the sale of excess electricity will provide enough profit to enable the East Millinocket mill to reopen.

A few retired engineers, with GNP roots, weeks before the announcement, started to quietly work on an informal plan to improve the East Millinocket mill's condition. The significance of the plan was not what it contained, but that the people who formulated it were not seeking financial remuneration; they wanted to help. The current employees have worked tirelessly to keep the mill running and producing quality paper, but have been largely unable to overcome the years of insufficient capital investment that stemmed an enduringly poor business climate.

The January 23rd announcement adds another potentially dark economic cloud to the skies of Katahdin, but we never know when the sun may shine through. There is a precedent for ceasing operations, because of economic losses that stem from production of a product, before a new business plan is completed. Henry Ford was forced to shut down his automotive operations in 1927, because he was losing money on every Model T sold. Production was halted for months as Ford retooled for the Model A. The Model A was very successful and Ford Motor Company remains in operation today.

Appendix A

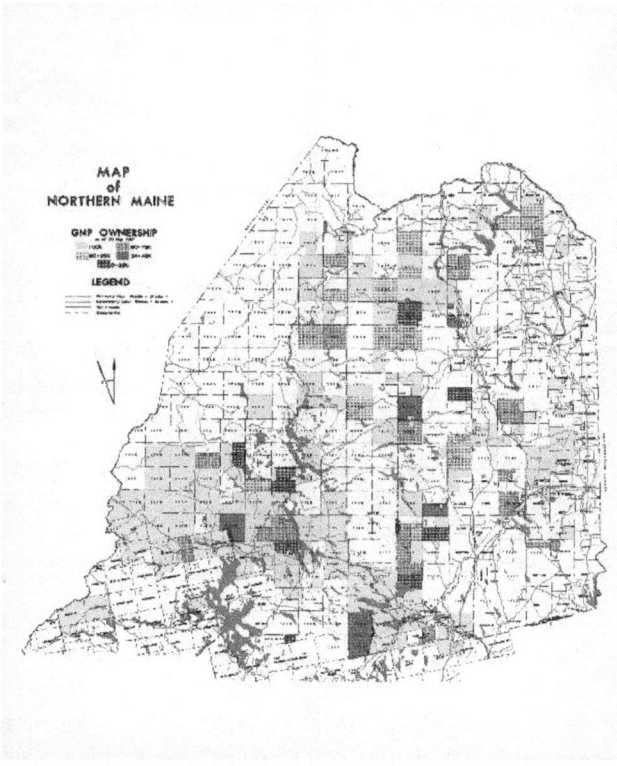

Figure 1: Internal Great Northern Paper map from May 1987 showing GNP's land ownership in Northern Maine. Light gray areas show entire townships with 100 percent ownership. Darker shaded areas show townships with less than 100 percent ownership. Compare these land holdings to the location of Millinocket and East Millinocket, the East and West Branches of the Penobscot River and the Railroad in figure two. GNP originally owned Mt. Katahdin (Maine's highest peak) and most of the land that now makes up Baxter State Park.

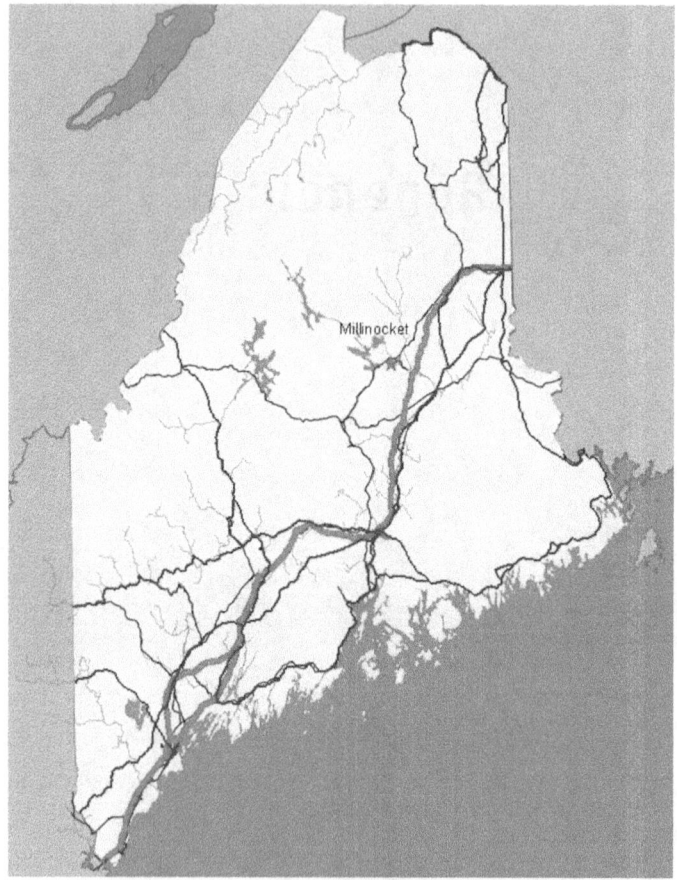

Figure 2: Map of Maine showing the location of Millinocket with a star. Notice the strategic location of the town in relation to the East and West branch of the Penobscot River. The heavy-gray line is Interstate 95. The light line, which extends east from Quebec and then branches northeast through Millinocket toward Houlton, is the railroad that enabled GNP to transport finished paper to market (when the mill in Millinocket was built, the railroad was the only form of transportation into town). It is also worth noting that to this day there are no towns located to the north or west of Millinocket.

Figure 3: A pre-1980s photo of the massive Millinocket mill. Note Millinocket stream in the foreground, the Engineering and Research building in the far right, the famous Number 11 is located in the silver colored building (without smoke stacks) on the left and Ferguson Pond in the upper left.

Figure 4: A pre-1980s photo of GNP's East Millinocket mill. Note the wood pile in the upper right and the pulp wood in the Penobscot River. The location of where the recycle plant was constructed in the early 1990s is not shown in this photo. The modernizations that occurred in the 1950s and 1980s were instrumental in the mills continued operations.

Figure 5: A July 2013 photo of the Millinocket mill showing massive amounts of the original complex in various stages of demolition. Previous owners had removed all of the paper machines but Number Eleven (long building on far right). A few other buildings remain, including the old grinding room, which has turbines that generate electricity. Note the canal in the foreground: The long building at the head of the canal is the gate house that controls the water going into the penstocks; the water runs underground from the gates, an approximate 110-foot drop in elevation, into the grinding room to generate electricity and then exits into Millinocket Stream.

Appendix B

Figure 1: A photo showing a 1918 Chevrolet 490. The 490 was one of the most important cars in GM's history. When William Durant, co-founder of Chevrolet, introduced the 490 in January of 1915, it became an instant sales success. It propelled Chevrolet's sales from less than two thousand to over twenty thousand, and with profits of over $1.3 million. Durant used his knowledge of the stock market and his skills as a master salesman to capitalize on the success of Chevrolet by acquiring shares of GM. By May of 1915, Durant announced that Chevrolet owned 54.4 percent of General Motors outstanding shares; in other words Chevrolet bought GM (Wright). Chevrolet remained a separate corporation until Durant folded it into GM in 1918 (Seaman). The success of the 490 was instrumental in Durant regaining control of GM. More importantly, it was Durant's success with Chevrolet that enabled him to purchase Hyatt Roller Bearing Company from Alfred P Sloan (forming United Motors,

a collection of parts suppliers, in 1916). When United Motors was integrated into GM, Sloan became a vice president of GM. Sloan later became CEO of GM, and his influence and contribution to the automobile industry was as significant as Henry Ford's.

Figure 2: A photo showing a 1916 Ford Model T. The Model T was produced from 1908 to 1927; it remains one of the most significant cars in American history, because it motorized America. The Model T made Ford the leading automobile producer in the world. The cars were originally designed and produced without an oil pump, water pump and fuel pump. The Model T's engine had a splash system that flung the oil as the crankshaft rotated as opposed to modern cars that have a pressurized oil pump. The coolant circulated via thermosyphon (hot water rises to the top of the motor and is replaced by cooler water from the radiator). The fuel was gravity fed from the tank to the carburetor (if a car couldn't climb a hill, the driver would have to turn around and back up the hill). The T's also had a two-speed transmission that operated with a pedal on the floor instead of a gearshift. It remained simple with limited changes throughout its production run. As a side note, the early Model T Fords had an impression where a driver's door would go but didn't have a door that would open (the driver had to enter from the passenger side.) Early Model Ts produced in Canada did have a functioning driver's door.

When Durant introduced the 490 with a three-speed transmission, electric lights and starter, Ford's answer was to lower the price of the Model T. Ford eventually produced T's with electric lights and starters, but the initial reaction of cutting the price instead of redesigning or modernizing the car proved to be a flaw that contributed to Ford losing its sales supremacy in 1928. Ford's strategy was not unlike the rebate wars of the late 1990s and early 2000s; both had similar results.

Bibliography

Adams, Glenn. "Big 'A' Dam Plan Is Still Alive, Says Great Northern Paper." *Lewiston Daily Sun.* January 10, 1986: 2.

Arnold, Ron, and Alan Gottlieb. *Trashing The Economy.* Bellevue: Free Enterprise Press, 1994.

Associated Press (AP). "Brennan Raps LURC 'Mistake' on Big 'A' Permit Conditions." *Bangor Daily News.* December 20, 1985: 1+.
————. "Personal Savings Drop to a 73-Year Low." *NBCNEWS.com.* February 1, 2007. http://www.msnbc.msn.com/id/16922582/ns/business-stocks_and_economy/t/personal-savings-drop--year-low/#.UCm-8qPUQZ4 (accessed August 13, 2012).
————. "US Savings Rate Hits Lowest Level Since 1933." *NBCNEWS.com.* January 30, 2006. http://www.msnbc.msn.com/id/11098797/ns/business-stocks_and_economy/t/us-savings-rate-hits-lowest-level/#.UCm-K6PUQZ4 (accessed August 13, 2012).

AutomotiveNews. "Rattner: GM and Chrysler Were a Mess." October 26, 2009. http://www.autonews.com/article/20091026/OEM02/310269862.

Baldwin, Clare, and Soyoung Kim. "GM IPO Raises $20.1 Billion." *Reuters.com.* November 17, 2010. http://www.reuters.com/article/2010/11/17/us-gm-ipo-idUSTRE6AB43H20101117 (accessed June 27, 2012).

Bangor Daily News. "Great Northern Earnings Up 10 Percent A Share." February 15, 1979. p23.

Barofsky, Neil. *Bailout.* New York: Free Press, 2012.

Barringer, Richard. *A Maine Manifest.* Portland, Maine: Tower Publishing Company, 1972.

Blagden, Nellie. "Lawyer Tom Tureen Has Bad News for Maine: the Indians Want, and May Get, Most of the State." *People.* January 31, 1977. http://www.people.com/people/archive/article/0,,20067374,00.html (accessed April 24, 2012).

Bomey, Nathan. "Former GMAC Puts Mortgage Unit In Bankruptcy." *USA Today*, May 14, 2012. http://content.usatoday.com/communities/driveon/post/2012/05/auto-bailout-ex-gmac-puts-mortgage-unit-in-bankruptcy/1#.Ua_6g5wSoTV

Bunyak, John, and Sandra V. Silva. "United States Department of the Interior." *Letter to Marc Cone, Maine Departmentof Environmental Protecton.* Denver: United States Department of the Interior, July 28, 2000.

Bush, George H.W. *Agenda for American Renewal.* Campaign Proposal, Bush-Quayle 1992 Election Committee, 1992.

Business Legislation Committee. *Study Report on Rate Making in Workers' Compensation.* Legislative Committee Report, Augusta: Business Legislation Committee, 1982.

Carson, James (town site manager, retired). Interview by M.J. Murphy. June 21, 2012.

CBC News. "CBC News In Depth: Kyoto and Beyond." *CBC.com.* February 14, 2007. http://www.cbc.ca/news/background/kyoto/ (accessed August 1, 2012).

Chide, Charles. "Smith Battles Sloan's Legacy." *Automotive News.* March 31, 1997: 25.

Churchill, Winston. *The Churchill Society London.* October 21, 1940. http://www.churchill-society-london.org.uk/LaFrance.html (accessed August 16, 2012).

Cleaves, Herb. "Maine Lands Bureau to Plan Public Lots." *Bangor Daily News.* August 26, 1981: 8.

Colias, Mike. "A CEO Search, GM Style, Who'll Take It?" *autonews. com.* January 28, 2013. http://www.autonews.com/apps/pbcs.dll/ article?AID=/20130128/OEM02/301289966/a-ceo-search-gm-style-wholl-take-it#axzz2KqBP2lOx (accessed February 20, 2013).

———. "GM's New Product Cycle: Fix Problems Now." *Automotive News.* April 1, 2013: http://www.autonews.com/ apps/pbcs.dll/article?AID=/20130401/OEM03/304019962/ gms-new-product-cycle-fix-problems-now#axzz2PGAkfro5.

———. "CFO Says GM Streamlining Is 'On Its Way.'" *Automotive News.* May 20, 2013: http://www.autonews.com/ apps/pbcs.dll/article?AID=/20130520/OEM02/305209994/ cfo-says-gm-streamlining-is-on-its-way#axzz2UpjgUU8h

———. "GM Taps Manufacturing Exec To Reduce Bureaucracy." *Automotive News.* June, 10 2013. http://www.autonews.com/ apps/pbcs.dll/article?AID=/20130610/OEM02/130619990/ gm-taps-manufacturing-exec-to-reduce-bureaucracy#axzz2WLbYkzi2

Conlogue, Eugene J. *Correspondence Related to National Park Service Interference with GNP Air Emisssions License Amendments in 2000.* Memo to Town Council from Eugene J. Conlogue, Town Manager, Millinocket: Town of Millinocket, 2011.

Dicenties, John (union president). Interview by M.J. Murphy. April 18, 2012.

Doody, Eldon (mill manager, former). Interview by M.J. Murphy. September 13, 2013.

Drogin, Bob. "'Civil War' Raging in Maine Woods, Big Employer Says Rapids Must Be
Dammed to Save Jobs." *Los Angeles Times.* July 23, 1985.

Edmans, Alex. "How to Fix Executive Compensation." *Wall Street Journal.* February 27, 2012. http://online.wsj.com/article/SB100014240529702 03462304577138691466777460.html.

Eilperin, Juliet, and Steven Mufson. "Artic Drilling Close for Shell, but Still Elusive." *Washington Post.* July 20, 2012. http://www.washingtonpost.

com/national/health-science/arctic-drilling-close-for-shell-but-still-elusive/2012/07/20/gJQATHdRyW_story.html?hpid=z3.

Epstein, Lita. "Is Mark-To-Market Accounting Rule Driving Financial Crisis?" *Daily Finance.* March 12, 2009. (accessed June 1, 2013). http://www.dailyfinance.com/2009/03/12/is-mark-to-market-accounting-rule-driving-financial-crisis/

Fish, Kelsey. (power systems superintendant, retired). Interview by M.J. Murphy. October 26, 2013.

Flint, Jerry. "The Ultimate Car Guy Parks it." *Forbes.com.* March 3, 2010. http://www.forbes.com/2010/03/03/bob-lutz-general-motors-business-autos-gm-lutz_2.html (accessed June 30, 2012).

Ford Motor Company. "Alan Mulally." *Media.Ford.com.* June 2011. http://media.ford.com/article_display.cfm?article_id=24203/ (accessed June 24, 2012).

Francis, Theo. "Fanny, Freddie Housing Goals May Exclude Subprime (Update 2)." *Bloomberg.com,* February 17, 2010: http://www.bloomberg.com/apps/news?pid=newsarchive&sid=aeXge2gVJGug.

Frick, Ali. "GM CEO: Serious Health Care Reform 'Undoubtedy Would Help Level The Playing Field.'" *Think Progress.* December 5, 2008. http://thinkprogress.org/politics/2008/12/05/33286/gm-health-care-reform/ (accessed June 13, 2012).

General Motors. *GM Quick Reference: The General Motors Quick Reference Site. GM.com.* 2010. http://media.gm.com/product/public/us/en/gmfacts/history/leadership.html#Bradley (accessed June 28, 2012).

Geng, Diane. "GM vs. Toyota By the Numbers." *NPR Business.* December 19, 2005. http://www.npr.org/news/specials/gmvstoyota/ (accessed August 30, 2012).

Georgia-Pacific Corporation, et al., Plaintiffs v. Great Northern Nekoosa, et al., Defendants. United States District Court for the District of Maine. February 15, 1990.

Gerow, Phil. "Trip to Georgia-Pacific Mills in the South Brings Mixed News." *Bangor Daily News.* August 24, 1990: 9.

Giffune, Jim (vice president GNP, retired). Interview by M.J. Murphy. December 21, 2011.

Grant, Phil, PhD. Hon DBA, interview by M. J. Murphy. *Professor* (March 21, 2013).

Greimel, Hans. "GM Had Early Start in Japan but Was Hobbled by Nationalism." *Automotive News.* September 15, 2008: 78.

Griffin, Tom (production manager, retired). Interview by M.J. Murphy. March 22, 2013.

Hall, Kevin G, McClatchy Newspapers. "SEC Sues Former Fannie and Freddie Execs For Fraud." *Bangor Daily News.* April 10, 2013.

Healey, James R. "GM Sells Majority Of Financing Unit." *USA Today,* April 7, 2006. http://usatoday30.usatoday.com/money/autos/2006-04-03-gm-deal_x.htm#.UanfjYAkqQI.email

Healey, James R., and Sharon Silke Carty. "GM-UAW Reach Tentative Deal: Strike Ends." *USA Today.* September 27, 2007.

Henderson, Frederick, A. Testimony delivered to United States House of Representatives Subcommittee for Oversite and Investigations, Subcommittee on Energy and Commerce. Washington, DC, June 12, 2009.

Henry, Jim. "Roger Smith's Diversification Strategy Created Saturn— and Lots of Problems." *Automotive News.* September 15, 2008: 222.

Kirsher, Tom, Dee-Ann Durbin, and Dan Strumpf. "GM CEO Ed Whitacre Jr. Will STEP DOWN, Automaker Posts $1.3 Billion Profit." *Huffington Post/Associated Press.* May 25, 2011. http://www.huffingtonpost. com/2010/08/12/gm-ceo-ed-whitacre-step-down_n_679690.html (accessed June 27, 2012).

Irwin Jr., Clark T. "Workers' Comp: Insurers Want Even Higher Premiums in Maine." *Portland Press Harold.* January 20, 1984.

Isidore, Chris. "GM IPO Biggest Ever." *CNN.com.* November 18, 2010. http://money.cnn.com/2010/11/17/news/companies/gm_ipo_pricing/index.htm (accessed June 27, 2012).

Jackson, Kathy. "Bitter Strike Gave Birth to the UAW, Created New Industrial Middle Class." *Automotive News.* September 15, 2008: 104.
———. "Health care: From Benefit to Crisis." *Automotive News.* September 15, 2008: 108.

Jeffs, Daniel B. "Who is responsible for this mortgage/financial train wreck?" *Direct Democracy Center.* October 3, 2008. http://www.realdemocracy.com/trainrek.htm (accessed April 11, 2013).

Johnson, Robert, PhD (manager of process design group). Interview by M.J. Murphy. July 12, 2012.

Khimm, Suzy. "No, the affordable housing push didn't cause the subprime crisis." *The Washington Post,* March 29, 2012: http://www.washingtonpost.com/blogs/wonkblog/post/no-the-affordable-housing-push-didnt-cause-the-subprime-crisis/2012/03/29/gIQADZ4YjS_blog.html

Kisiel, Ralph. "GM's 0 Percent Financing Helped Calm a Nervous Nation after 9/11." *Automotive News.* September 15, 2008: 276.

Korzeniewski, Jeremy. "Mark LaNeve Leaving GM Effective October 15." *Autoblog.com.* October 7, 2009. http://www.autoblog.com/2009/10/07/breaking-mark-laneve-reportedly-leaving-gm-effective-october-15/ (accessed June 30, 2012).

LaReau, Jamie. "After the Frenetic Durant Era, Sloan Brought Order From Chaos." *Automotive News.* September 15, 2008: 64.
———. "900,000 Orphans: GM Risks Loosing Loyal Customers As It Whacks Small-Town Dealerships." *Automotive News,* October 5, 2009: 1+.

Lawder, David. "GM, AIG Shares Slide to Add $23 Billion to Deficit." *Reuters.com.* Jan 31, 2012. http://www.reuters.com/article/2012/01/31/us-usa-budget-tarp-idUSTRE80U2K620120131 (accessed July 5, 2012).

Laverty, Dorthy. *Millinocket Magic City of Maine's Wilderness.* Freeport: The Bond Wheelwright Company, 1973.

Legasse, Mary Anne. "Bowater May Sell All Maine Holdings." *Bangor Daily News.* July 10, 1998: 1-.
————. "GNP Power Sale Finished; Canadian Group buys Dams, Stations." *Bangor Daily News.* Feb 2, 2002.

Lobozzo, Allan. "Legislation Has Favored Workers' Compensation: Maine Summer Labor Institute Hears Supporter." *Bangor Daily News.* August 24, 1984.

Lousiana Pacific. "State of Maine." *Maine Department of Transportation Website.* September 2, 2009. http://www.maine.gov/mdot/tigergrants/ntrpp/documents/lpc.pdf (accessed April 10, 2012).

Lutz, Bob. *Car Guys vs. Bean Counters: The Battle for the Soul of American Business.* New York: Penguin Group, 2011.
————. *Straight Talk On Leadership: Icons And Idiots.* New York: Penguin Group, 2013.

Maine legislature 1983. LD 1721. *An Act to Promote the Wise Use and Management of Maine's Outstanding River Resources.* Augusta, July 17, 1983.

Mateja, Jim. "Reputation Only Style Top-Selling Camry Needs." *Chicago Tribune.* February 27, 2005. http://articles.chicagotribune.com/2005-02-27/travel/0502270280_1_awd-toyota-camry-hybrid.

McCann, Paul K. *Timber: The Fall of Maine's Paper Giant.* Ellsworth: Ellsworth American, 1994.

Meriturn Partners. *Meriturn Withdraws From Katahdin Acquistion.* April 8, 2011. http://www.meriturn.com/news/?id=149 (accessed April 13, 2012).

Morgan, Dan. *Nospeedbumps.com.* December 21, 2005. http://nospeedbumps.com/?p=606 (accessed 6 13, 2012).

Morrison, Frederic (town site manager, retired). Interview by M.J. Murphy. July 13, 2012.

Nader, Ralph. *Unsafe at Any Speed.* New York: Pocket Books, 1966.

Nelson, Gabe. "Study: GM, Chrysler Bailouts Generated 8-to-1 Savings." *Automotive News.* December 9, 2013: http://www.autonews.com/article/20131209/OEM/131209870/study-gm-chrysler-bailouts-generated-8-to-1-savings#

Pelfrey, William. *Billy, Alfred, and General Motors.* New York: AMACOM American Management Association, 2006.

Petre, Jonathan. "Climategate U-Turn as Scientist at Centre of Row Admits: There Has Been No Global Warming Since 1995." *Daily Mail Online.* February 14, 2010 (accessed July 30, 2012).

Pidwirny, M. "Atmospheric Composition." *Fundamentals of Physical Geography, 2nd Edition.*
http://www.physicalgeography.net/fundamentals/7a.html (accessed July 30, 2012).

Platt, David. "GNP Mulls the Options on Big 'A.'" *Bangor Daily News.* December 20, 1985: 1+.

Pray, Charles P. (president of the Maine state senate). Interview by M.J. Murphy. May 15, 2012.

Public Law LD 1322. "An Act to Reform the Workers' Compensation System." Augusta: 111th Maine legislature , 1983.

Rattner, Steven. *Overhaul.* Boston: Mariner Books, 2011.

Restore: the North Woods. *About Restore.* 2012. http://www.restore.org/Restore/mission.html (accessed May 24, 2012).

Richardson, Warren (plant manager, Leav River). Interview by M.J. Murphy. June 10, 2012.

Richardson, Whit. "Maine Sues Standard & Poor's, Alleges Deceptive Practices Led To '08 Financial Frisis." *Bangor Daily News.* February 5, 2013.

Roop, David (senior marketing analyst). Interview by M.J. Murphy. *Senior Marketing Analyst (retired)* (April 11, 2012).

Rosevear, John, and The Motley Fool, "Government Motors: Why Won't D.C. Sell Its GM Stock?" *DailyFinance.com*. March 28, 2012. http://www. dailyfinance.com/2012/03/28/gm-government-motors-washington-obama-tarp-stock/ (accessed July 5, 2012).

Sambides Jr., Nick. "Katahdin Mills Anticipate Progress." *Bangor Daily News*. May 7, 2007: A4.
———. "Katahdin Paper Mill to Stay Open Beyond July 28 Shutdown Date." *Bangor Daily News*. July 10, 2008: A1.
———. "New Law Gives Katahdin Mills Electric Priority." *Bangor Daily News*. April 6, 2010. http://bangordailynews.com/2010/04/06/news/ new-law-gives-katahdin-mills-electric-priority/?ref=search
———. "Mills' Buyer Seeks $48 Million in Town Tax Breaks." *Bangor Daily News*. March 1, 2011. http://bangordailynews.com/2011/03/01/ business/mills%E2%80%99-buyer-seeks-48m-in-town-tax-breaks/?ref=relatedBox.
———. "East Millinocket Mill Closes as Katahdin Paper Mills' Sale Negotiations Halt." *Bangor Daily News*. April 08, 2011: 1.

Sanabe and Associates, LLC. *Sanabe.com*. http://www.sanabe.com/docs/ Bowater-Case-Study.pdf (accessed April 7, 2012).

Seaman, Kirk. "Roger Smith's Grand Plan: Unravel Division System, Create a Unified GM." *Automotive News*. September 15, 2008: 230.
———. "To Get Back in the Race for GM, Durant Found a Racer." *Automotive News*. September 15, 2008: 40.

Sherman, Roger (director). *Chevy 100: An American Story*. Performed by Chevrolet Motor Division. 2011.

Shunk, Chris. "Report: TARP Audit Criticizes Obama Task Force for Dealer Closings." *Autoblog.com*. July 19, 2010. http://www.autoblog. com/2010/07/19/report-tarp-audit-criticizes-obama-task-force-for-dealer-closin/ (accessed June 30, 2012).

Sloan, Alfred P. Jr. *My Years With General Motors*. New York: Currency Doubleday, 1990.

Slocum, Peter. "Session Fails to End Paper Strike." *Lewiston Evening Journal*. August 23, 1978: 7.

Smith, George. "Trotting out Trotzky at the Maine Legislature." *DownEast.com.* February 17, 2012, http://www.downeast.com/georges-outdoor-news/2012/february/trotting-maine-legislature (accessed April 21, 2012).

Sorge, Marge. "Contracts and Controversary." *Automotive News.* September 16, 1983 (GM's 75th Anniversary Issue): 351-62.

Speaker's Select Committee on Workers' Compensation. *Report of Speaker's Select Committee on Workers' Compensation.* Speaker of the House John L. Martin's Workers' Compensation Committee, Augusta: State House, 1983.

State of Maine Board of Environmental Protection. *In the Matter of: Great Northern Paper, Inc., PSD Air Emission License A-406-71-W-A.* Appeal of the United States Department of the Interior from Issuance of the License, Augusta: Maine Board of Environmental Protection, 2000.

Maine State Planning Office. *Maine.gov.* May 21, 2012. http://www.maine.gov/spo/about/index.htm (accessed May 21, 2012).

Teahen Jr., John K. "Strong Dealer Organization, Based on Buick Model, Kept Metal Moving." *Automotive News.* September 15, 2008: 80.

Texas Comptroller of Public Accounts. "Window on State Government." TCPA website. http://www.window.state.tx.us/specialrpt/energy/renewable/hydro.php (accessed May 16, 2012).

The Employee Benefit Research Institute. 2010 Retirement Confidence Survey—2010 Results. *Ebri.com.* March 9, 2010. http://www.ebri.org/pdf/surveys/rcs/2010/FS-03_RCS-10_Prep.pdf (accessed August 13, 2012).

Thomas, Ken. "US Task Force Shocked by State of GM, Chrysler." *USA Today.* October 21, 2009. http://www.usatoday.com/money/autos/2009-10-21-auto-task-force_N.htm (accessed June 30, 2012).

Thompson, Arthur A. Jr., and A.J. Strickland. "Strategic Management: Concepts and Cases, 8th Edition." In *The World Automotive Industry in 1994,* by Arthur A. Jr. Thompson and John E. Gamble, 512-560. Chicago: Irwin, 1995.

Turcotte, Deborah. "Katahdin Paper Might Open Mill." *Bangor Daily News.* October 31, 2003: A9.

Turkel, Tux. "New State, New Baby, No Controversy for Maine Tribes Advocate." *Portland Press Herald.* March 15, 2010.

University of Southern Maine. "Muskie School of Public Policy." USM website. April 20, 2012, http://webapp.usm.maine.edu/MuskieWebDBfrontend/personView.action?personId=4 (accessed April 20, 2012).

Virginia Tech. "About Virginia Tech: Buildings." Virginia Tech website. http://www.vt.edu/about/buildings/graduate-life-center.html (accessed June 28, 2012).

Wallison, Peter J, and Edward J Pinto. "A Government-Mandated Housing Bubble." *Forbes.com,* February 2, 2009: http://www.forbes.com/2009/02/13/housing-bubble-subprime-opinions-contributors_0216_peter_wallison_edward_pinto.html.

Wernie, Bradford, and Mark Rechtin. "Jim Press Saga: A Hero Falls, Hard." *Automotive News.* October 26, 2009: 1+.

Will, George F. "What Ails GM." *Washington Post.* May 1, 2005. http://www.washingtonpost.com/wp-dyn/content/article/2005/04/29/AR2005042901385.html.

Woodbury, David. "The Fall of Great Northern Paper." *Damnyankee.com.* June 2005. http://www.damnyankee.com/page89/page1/page63/fall_of_GNP.html (accessed April 7, 2012).

Wright, Richard A. "The Durant Years." *Automotive News.* September 16, 1983: 21-29.

Ziegler, Jim. "Dealer Advocate." *Dealer Magazine.* November 2009: 12+.

Index

www.ingramcontent.com/pod-product-compliance
Lightning Source LLC
Chambersburg PA
CBHW071422170526
45165CB00001B/357